FINAL WARNING

UNDERSTANDING THE TRUMPET DAYS OF REVELATION

CARL GALLUPS

WND Books

FINAL WARNING

Copyright © 2014 by Carl Gallups

Published by WND Books®, Washington, D.C. WND Books is a registered trademark of WorldNetDaily.com, Inc. ("WND")

Book designed by Mark Karis

WND Books are distributed to the trade by:
Midpoint Trade Books, 27 West 20th Street, Suite 1102, New York, New York 10011
WND Books are available at special discounts for bulk purchases. WND Books, Inc., also publishes books in electronic formats. For more information call (541) 474-1776 or visit www.wndbooks.com.

Paperback ISBN: 978-1-938067-61-7   eBook ISBN: 978-1-938067-62-4

Library of Congress Cataloging-in-Publication Data
Gallups, Carl, 1955-
Final warning : are we living in the trumpet days of revelation? / Carl Gallups.
pages cm
Includes bibliographical references.
ISBN 978-1-938067-61-7 (hardcover)
1. Bible. Revelation--Criticism, interpretation, etc. I. Title.
BS2825.52.G35 2015
228.06--dc23
2014029613

Printed in the United States of America
15 16 17 18 19 EBM 9 8 7 6 5 4

TO MY FELLOW PILGRIMS
at HICKORY HAMMOCK BAPTIST CHURCH
in MILTON, FLORIDA.

And the angel took the censer, and filled it with fire of the altar, and cast it into the earth: and there were voices, and thunderings, and lightnings, and an earthquake. And the seven angels which had the seven trumpets prepared themselves to sound.

—REVELATION 8:5–6

A WATCHMAN

Son of man, speak to the children of thy people, and say unto them, When I bring the sword upon a land, if the people of the land take a man of their coasts, and set him for their watchman: if when he seeth the sword come upon the land, he blow the trumpet, and warn the people; then whosoever heareth the sound of the trumpet, and taketh not warning; if the sword come, and take him away, his blood shall be upon his own head. He heard the sound of the trumpet, and took not warning; his blood shall be upon him. But he that taketh warning shall deliver his soul. But if the watchman see the sword come, and blow not the trumpet, and the people be not warned; if the sword come, and take any person from among them, he is taken away in his iniquity; but his blood will I require at the watchman's hand.

—EZEKIEL 33:2–6

And the third angel sounded, and there fell a great star from heaven, burning as it were a lamp, and it fell upon the third part of the rivers, and upon the fountains of waters; and the name of the star is called Wormwood: and the third part of the waters became wormwood; and many men died of the waters, because they were made bitter.

—REVELATION 8:10–11

The sad illustration of this is the Chernobyl catastrophe. It happened on the territory of my country, where—rephrasing the Revelation of St. John the Divine—"a great star fell from heaven upon the third part of the rivers." Although it occurred more than a decade ago, the "Chernobyl star of Wormwood" still hovers like a Damoclean sword over the world and as a bitter reminder for all of us.

—HENNADIY UDOVENKO, Minister for Foreign Affairs of Ukraine, during his inaugural address as president of the fifty-second session of the General Assembly of the United Nations (September 16, 1997)

CONTENTS

ACKNOWLEDGMENTS

To my wonderful and loving wife, Pam, with whom I have been in love since I was sixteen and without whom none of my books would have been written. You are truly the Lord's gift and blessing to my life.

I am grateful to the wonderful people of Hickory Hammock Baptist Church in Milton, Florida. You called me to be your pastor and fellow pilgrim in 1987. It is my honor to continue to advance the Kingdom of Jesus Christ with you. May the Lord bless you and keep you—always.

I am deeply grateful to my research assistants, Brandon (Big

B) Gallups and Mike Shoesmith whose work and enthusiasm was invaluable to me during the pre-writing process.

To my son, Brandon, my daughter-in-law, Hannah, and my grandson, Parker, I am so proud of each of you. Thank you for your encouragement.

To West Side Baptist Church, Jasper, Alabama—under the leadership of Dr. Fred Lackey – thank you for allowing me to proclaim among you the wonders of Revelation and end-time prophecy for five years straight. May God richly bless you.

As with most years-long projects there are many important people who have helped me with this book and/or have greatly encouraged my writing ministry along the way. Thank you Dr. Dennis Brunet, Rev. Brad Lowery, Rev. Tim Bullington, Dr. Mark Foley, Dr. Lucky Teage, Dr. David Reagan, Dr. Chuck Kelley, Dr. Greg Robards, Dr. Jack Goldfarb and his wife Bonnie, Rev. Jim Rinehart, Amie Morrell, Joanne Parker, Dr. Joda Collins, Rev. Jeff Keeman, Dr. Grace Vuoto (World Tribune), Jeff Kuhner (WRKO), Jerry McGlothlin (SpecialGuests.com), Bill Martinez (*Bill Martinez Live*), Lori Roth (*The Lori Roth Show*), Mike LeMay (*Stand Up For Truth* – WORQ), Greg Burnley, Carl Lamm (WTSB), Zev Porat (Messiah of Israel Ministries), Mike Bates, and the staff of 1330 WEBY AM, and Lou Vickery (WPFL).

I am indebted to my parents, Bill and Holly Gallups, who have encouraged me all my life. Thank you, Dad and Mom.

And to my wife's parents, Nelson and Marlene Blount, thank you; I could not ask for more encouraging and loving in-laws.

Finally, a special word of appreciation goes to my publisher WND Books. Their tireless dedication to excellence continues to be a blessing and inspiration to me. My deepest thanks to Joseph Farah, Elizabeth Farah, Michael Thompson, Mark Karis, Geoffrey Stone, Kelsey Whited, Renee Chavez, and the tremendous WND Books and WND.com staff.

INTRODUCTION
STARTLING PROPHETIC QUESTIONS OF OUR TIMES

What a time to take the news of the day in one hand and the Bible in the other and watch the unfolding of the great drama of the ages come together.

—DR. BILLY GRAHAM[1]

Jesus told His disciples that in the time of the end, they need not worry. He assured them He would send His angels with *a great sound of a trumpet* and with that unparalleled trumpet blast, He would gather His elect from over the face of the earth (Matt. 24:31). Many believe our generation might be on the cusp of that portentous day.

But, could it be that we are now living in the specific "trumpet prophecy" days spoken of in the New Testament book of Revelation? Are certain biblical end-time prophecies truly unfolding before our eyes and lining up with world-renowned historical events?

Are there credible connections between the well-known Chernobyl nuclear disaster of 1986 and the wormwood prophecy outlined in John's third trumpet vision in Revelation 8?

What about reports that the biblical words *Abaddon* and *Apollyon* in Revelation 9 match up perfectly with the ancient Persian word *Saddam* . . . as in Saddam Hussein?

Are violently burning oil wells mentioned in Revelation? Was Saddam's five-month uncontested occupation of Kuwait foretold thousands of years ago? Or are these speculations merely unwarranted stretching of biblical visions made to "fit" current events?

Is there anything in history that would correspond with the vision of the second trumpet that describes something like a giant mountain, all ablaze, thrown into the sea?

Is there any reliably documented science that proves the earth has experienced a dimming of light—as described in the fourth-trumpet prophecy?

Does the Bible actually speak of a rapture event—a catching away of God's people in the last days? If so, how is that occurrence tied to the trumpet prophecies of Revelation?

Are the seven feasts of the Lord tied to end-time prophecy and, specifically, to the prophecies?

Is the United States relevant to biblical prophecy? If we are actually living in the biblical last days, would there not be at least a veiled reference to the United States? This question is often asked since the United States is undoubtedly the world's foremost superpower. Because of its prominence in world affairs, the United States is directly tied to Israel's existence and protection, as well as its standing in Middle Eastern political affairs. And, indisputably, Israel and the Middle East are linked to biblical end-time markers.

Do the rise of Islam, Islamic terrorism, and the Arab Spring have any accurate biblical connections—especially concerning end-time prophecy?

Are monumental and world-renowned events such as World War I, World War II, the Chernobyl disaster, the Gulf War, the

9/11 terror attacks, the Arab Spring, and the current upheaval in the Middle East actually connected prophetically? Furthermore, do these events have key word associations encoded within the plain text of the Scriptures' end-time prophecies?

You will discover the potential answers to these and so many more questions within the pages of this book.

An incredible journey of contextual biblical understanding and astounding prophetic possibilities awaits you.

AUTHOR'S NOTE

The scripture passages quoted in this book are presented in two different formats. In shorter sections, where a particular biblical truth is simply being pointed out, the scripture is represented in paragraph form. In the longer passages, those scriptures are displayed verse by verse. Using the two different formats makes for overall ease of reading and better clarity of the subject matter at hand.

Three Bible translations are used throughout the book: the King James Version, the New American Standard Version, and the New International Version. In each case, I selected the version that best represents the most literal translation, balanced with ease of reading, for the particular passage quoted.

Obviously, even considering the possibility that we might be living in the Revelation "trumpet prophecy days" requires that the prophecy student hold a mid-tribulation to post-tribulation rapture view, and certainly a pre-wrath view. The pre-tribulation rapture understanding postulates that the trumpet vision events of Revelation happen *after* the rapture of the church. Several of the important differences in these views will be addressed as we advance with this study.

As of this writing, I have been the senior pastor of one church since 1987. The congregation there can attest that I am not known as a preacher of "hype." I am not an alarmist or "date-setter." My number one goal in life is simply to advance the kingdom of Jesus

Christ and to contextually proclaim the Word of God while highlighting the foundational fundamentals of the faith.

Those foundational teachings are: Jesus is God with us and our only way of salvation; the Bible is the infallible, all-sufficient, and final Word of God, and when interpreted contextually, all truth may be rightly divided by that Word. And finally, salvation is gained by God's grace alone through faith alone. From these great truths there can be no wavering.

Conversely, there are other areas of biblical understanding that are not as foundational as the fundamentals of which I have just spoken. Eschatology is one of those areas. The Bible simply does not give us a black-and-white, chart-by-the-numbers blueprint of the exact timing of last-days events.

However, we *are* able to discern the seasons and the times in which we live. Jesus scolded those in His day who could not "discern the signs of the times" (Matt. 16:1–3). We are also charged with proclaiming the great and clear prophetic truths of the Word of God. On the other hand, to declare that one must believe every line and nuance of a certain eschatological scenario is a dangerous road upon which to tread.

If you do not believe me, please consider the horrific blunders of the Pharisees. They insisted they had every jot and tittle of eschatology figured out. But they were so wrong that they actually arranged for the crucifixion of God's Son—all in the name of their "figured out" eschatology! Jesus Himself did not fit into their predetermined and rigid scenario of end-time and messianic happenings!

Often, if a consistently solid exegetical explorer comes to a different conclusion concerning an otherwise popular belief, he or she is branded as a *heretic*. Since *heresy* is frequently defined as "doctrinal error"—I suppose we all could be branded as heretics at one time or another. Think about it . . . have you always been 100 percent correct in your doctrinal understanding and pronouncements? Would you dare to proclaim that you are currently 100 percent correct in your interpretation about every doctrinal issue in the Bible? Is there any room at all for your biblical understanding to be contextually tweaked or corrected?

And then there is this argument: *Well, the majority of reliable scholars say you are wrong about your understanding in this matter of eschatology.* I admit this protestation can often serve as a warning, indicating that perhaps one might be off the biblical track. But this is not always the case.

Remember, Jesus stood alone against all those scholars—and the scholars were wrong. Practically every one of the now-revered biblical prophets stood alone against *all those scholars*. And again, the scholars were wrong. The apostle Paul regularly proclaimed absolute heresy, as far as his religious-elite peers were concerned, when he insisted that Jesus was the Christ. Nevertheless, he was right, and the scholars were wrong. The wise men from the East were willing to go against the accepted dogma of *all those scholars* of their day, and they found the Messiah . . . the scholars did not.

Dealing with prophecy from a balanced and plainly contextual point of understanding, while not merely giving heed to the latest and most popular fads, is not always the most comfortable undertaking. However, leaving room to be mistaken and to be contextually corrected, I press forward. I pray that you will also.

Our goal should be to let scripture interpret scripture . . . first and foremost. I want to know the biblical *truth* of the matter even if it upsets my previously held belief. I want to know what the Bible clearly says, in a contextual manner, regardless of popular belief, the most admired literature, or the most accepted interpretation of our times. Oh, if only the religious elite of Jesus' day would have desired such a thing!

* * *

I have been revealing the amazing discoveries set forth in this book since the beginning of my ministry. My observations have been candidly disclosed in revivals, conferences, video presentations, newspaper articles, and radio programs. My beliefs have not been hidden in a remote corner.

Over these many years, a number of people have implored me to write these things down in a book, and to document and credibly reference my findings. The task has been put off for years simply because I knew it would be a daunting one. However, through all those years the constant requests have gnawed at me until I was finally convinced, perhaps by the Spirit of God, that this book must be written.

So here it is. Prepare yourself for some revelations. Please read it to the end—even if it makes you a bit uncomfortable along the way. If you disagree with some of its material, you have not lost a thing except a few hours of your time. On the other hand, you may find that you have discovered some matters that will require further and serious pondering.

Our story begins where it must—downtown Ephesus, AD 95.

"Wrong will be right, when Aslan comes in sight,
At the sound of his roar, sorrows will be no more,
When he bares his teeth, winter meets its death,
And when he shakes his mane, we shall have spring again."
—C.S. LEWIS, *The Lion, the Witch, and the Wardrobe*

1
I, JOHN, WAS IN THE SPIRIT . . .

"The revelation of Jesus Christ, which God gave him to show
his servants what must soon take place. He made it known by
sending his angel to his servant John."

—REV. 1:1 NIV

The judicial chamber was elegantly appointed. Everything
about the place bespoke the sheer power and technological
prowess of the mighty Roman Empire of the first century
anno Domini.

The courtroom gallery was packed with Ephesian citizens,
mostly because of the presence of one particular man. The
humble, smallish, and elderly man was a rather prominent resident
of Ephesus—especially in certain religious circles. But today, he was
in desperate trouble with the Roman legal authorities.

One by one, the current docket of the criminal rabble was

brought before the judge. His Honor, an appointee of Rome, was prominently elevated—peering down, from on high, at the lowly throng. The *cognitio extra ordinem* (a special investigation ordered by the governor) had been completed.

The gang of the variously accused had been ushered into the room in clanging chains. Court attorneys and prosecutors scuttled about from client to client, incessantly chattering in hushed tones.

At the magistrate's sharp order, the elderly little Jew shuffled up in front of the judge's bench. A legal advocate accompanied him. Two guards stood at either side. After ten full minutes of his attorney's pleas for acquittal and then, finally, a plea for a display of mercy—the magistrate indicated that sentencing would be pronounced.

"You, John—pastor of the church at Ephesus, are hereby sentenced to *exile*—for the rest of your natural life!" Murmurs of delight erupted from among the gallery. John stood silent, as was required. He faced his judgment with honor, yet a deep sadness enveloped him.

For the rest of my life? How in the world will my congregation survive? What is to be my destiny for the kingdom work now? How can my life be made useful any longer for the sake of the gospel? His head throbbed with these questions he could not answer. His eyes welled with tears. The room became silent again. A few in the gallery nervously cleared their throats. The judge continued, as he adjusted the collar of his robe.

"On this venerated day, in the reign of our dear Emperor Domitian, *Dominus et Deus*—whom you, John, have *defiled* by your insolence, I sentence you to spend the rest of your life on Patmos island. You are never again to return to the good Roman society that you have so consistently spurned and so smugly disdained by your appalling disrespect! It is done and ordered! That is all!"

The gavel fell with a deafening crack. John submissively returned to his assigned spot and fell back into the rickety chair. He folded his hands, lowered his head, and silently prayed. His hands trembled. Hot tears splattered to the floor at his feet. His appointed lawyer ignored him and quickly scuttled over to the next client.

The guards approached John with chains and heavy iron shackles. As they drew near, the old man slowly lifted his head and willingly extended his arms for the restraints. *Somehow the Lord will provide,* John thought. *Somehow.*

John, the acclaimed gospel preacher of Ephesus, had been accused of being an anti-Emperor-worship activist. Being the most prominent figure of his cultic Jewish-Christian group, as the Romans called it, he had been specifically targeted and finally singled out by the authorities.

John's frequent protests concerning the sacrilege had been noticed by Rome itself. Domitian had become enraged by John's reputed influence over a sizable segment of the Ephesian citizenry. Emperor-appointed spies had been dispatched to Ephesus. John's arrest had been ordered directly from the Emperor's throne. This disrespectful throng of disgusting Christians had to be stopped.

The worst punishment reserved for criminals who were not sentenced to death was to strip them of their civil rights and to banish them to a remote corner of the empire. The Roman Empire had long ago designated the rocky, forlorn island of Patmos as one such spot of utter seclusion. A banishment sentence was dreaded, by many people of John's day, more than a death sentence—and the Romans knew it.

John had been accused of refusing to sacrifice a pig and obstinately declining to lay a worship tax of gold coins upon the altar of the imperial cult—the worship of Domitian. To refuse to participate in the forced pagan ritual was a capital crime, punishable by death or lifelong exile.

Emperor Titus Flavius Caesar Domitianus Augustus saw himself as the new Caesar Augustus, an enlightened autocrat predestined to direct the Roman Empire into a new era of civilized luminosity. The year was AD 95. Religious, military, and cultural propaganda fostered a growing and frenzied cult of personality surrounding Rome's new *god.*

By nominating himself perpetual censor, Domitian set out to manipulate and redirect public and private morals. As a consequence, the emperor was popular with the vast majority of the Roman people, especially the military. His senate was terrified of his unbridled power.

Domitian, relishing the authority he now wielded, became the first Roman emperor to *demand* to be addressed as *Dominus et Deus* (Master and God). He ensured that libelous writings, especially those specifically directed against him, were punishable by exile or death. As a result, large numbers of Jews and Christians suffered miserably under his tyranny.

The huge edifice of his sacrificial altar was located just to the south of the imperial town square in Ephesus. The ornate building had become the first temple of the imperial cult erected in the Roman province of Anatolia. Its presence wrought a devastating impact upon the Jewish and Christian culture within the city. Many had simply succumbed to the humiliation, rationalizing that *there was really no harm done in humoring the foolish Romans who thought their emperor was a god.*

The fact was a large number of Christians had flatly compromised; furthermore, they had grown comfortable in their compromise. John had tried to awaken them from their spiritual stupor and blasphemous practices. Now he would pay for his unswerving commitment to the purity of the gospel of Jesus Christ. And no one came to his defense. He was alone.

"The truth is . . . why should I be exempt?" John mumbled softly to himself. *"After all—every one of my brother apostles are now gone . . . I am the only one left. Peter, James, and Matthew—every one of them paid the ultimate price. Why not me as well? Why should I live to be such an old man?"* A faint smile formed upon his lips. He remembered the words of Jesus, spoken decades ago, "What if I decide that John should live until I come again?"

The next pronouncement of sentence ripped at John's heart. The prisoner's name was Prochorus. He was John's fiery young disciple who had stood with him in the defiant protest of the repulsive emperor worship. They had been arrested on the same day and had been held in the same cell awaiting this day of sentencing. They had clearly known the dangers of their actions, and John possessed no reservations about his own protests. But now . . . he watched in sorrow as Prochorus was shuffled before the judge's bench.

"Guilty!" The gavel crashed. The judge continued his sentencing with an austere voice: "You have followed your teacher's perverse and superstitious ways—now you may follow him to Patmos . . . for the rest of your natural life!" The judge shot a wicked glance in John's direction. "See, old man, what you have wrought upon this youthful life?" he accused. "How many more innocents will you destroy by your insolence? How much more anguish would you have willfully brought to your congregation?

"We simply will not tolerate, in this great city, a misguided religious insurrection against our dear emperor—not in Ephesus! *Dominus et Deus* will be honored among us! And I intend to lead the way. Perhaps others of your kind will learn the lesson of your sentence. Done and ordered! *Next!*"

"*Oh, God, have I done the right thing?*" John prayed in agony, silently. Never before had he been uncertain of his own actions. But now, a young man's future was over—*forever*. John's zeal had cost the boy dearly.

John felt a dash of reassurance when Prochorus turned from his sentencing, looked his old pastor squarely in the face—and smiled. The guards roughly fastened Prochorus's shackles and prepared him for delivery to Patmos. John thought: *Unless the Lord intervenes, we will never return to civilization. We may as well be dead to Ephesus, and our families and friends. Life, as we have known it, is over.*

John jumped, startled as the judge's gavel once again crashed down upon the desk. "*Next!*"

* * *

Within days of their sentencing, John and Prochorus arrived on Patmos along with a shipload of other unfortunates. Patmos was a quarry for the Roman Empire, and was now the eternal home to numerous political and religious prisoners and slaves. The island was rocky and desolate, except for the forbidding mammoth stone building that served as the main edifice for the officials who oversaw the mining work of the island.

The first few weeks on the island were practically unbearable. Food and shelter were scant. Civilized conduct among the island's residents was virtually nonexistent. But John and his young protégé adjusted. They had to—there was no other choice. They understood this must become their new mission field. The desperate souls on this island needed the Lord as much as anyone else—*anywhere* else.

To the angst of some of his fellow inmates, John led several to salvation in Jesus Christ. And he spent much of his time writing. He wrote of his past. He wrote of his times with Jesus. He chronicled the life, ministry, death, and resurrection of Jesus. He wrote these accounts for the benefit of those on the island, and also with the hope that perhaps—someday—he might be able to bribe someone to get his writings off the island and into the hands of the believers back in Ephesus. Young Prochorus often served as John's secretary and scribe.

Weeks turned into months; the months passed into years. As John grew older, he grew feebler. Prochorus had resigned himself to the fact that he would never leave the miserable island. He worked the mines by day—and ministered with John by night. Not surprisingly, under God's anointing, John eventually grew to become highly trusted by the island's Roman authorities.

John was unable to perform the manual labor the mines required, but the elderly pastor was a calming presence among the rest. So, he was allowed to wander about . . . and minister.

How ironic, John thought. *I was banished to this place for preaching the gospel and refusing to worship the emperor. But here, I am allowed to share the gospel, and rarely is the emperor's name even mentioned. God's ways certainly are not our ways!*

And he wrote:

Dear Matthias of Ephesus, I write this personal note to accompany the scroll of the Revelation, which I have received directly from our Lord Jesus Christ while on the island of Patmos. Truly, our Lord has visited me! I speak the absolute truth to you in this matter—I am not lying, nor have I gone mad! Please relate this letter, in full, to our brothers and sisters at the church of Ephesus as you deliver the scroll that is with it.

It was on a Lord's Day, a few months after my arrival upon Patmos, when the most amazing thing happened to me. It was a Sunday, as the Romans call it, the first day of the week. I stumbled into a small cave I had discovered only a few weeks earlier. This location had become for me a place of rest, seclusion, and prayer.

On that particular Sunday I made my way there to meditate upon the Word of our Lord and to pray. I looked around the dimly lit void, took a deep breath, and started to kneel so that I could lean against the wall. But all of a sudden, I was stopped. An alarming, deeply resonant noise erupted behind me. The din sounded as if it had come from within the cave's shadowy depths. Suddenly, the voice of it was everywhere. It was booming and splendid—it was inside and, at the same time, outside, like the sound of a shofar blasting through the hills of Judea! Then the voice evolved into intelligible words.

"Write!" the voice said. "Write in a book what you will see. Send your book to the seven churches of Anatolia!" My body began to tremble uncontrollably. I hesitated to turn to gaze upon the source of the voice behind me. Was it the Lord? I was certain I recognized the voice of our Lord! Had He come to Patmos? Had He come to me? Had He come to deliver us?

I took another deep breath. I gathered my nerves and slowly turned. And there He stood! Among a set of seven dazzlingly beautiful golden lampstands! He was clothed in pure, unadulterated, and brilliant light! The radiance of His glory filled the small cavern. The air sparkled with flecks of shimmering luminosity. His face was as bright as the sun itself, yet visible and recognizable, and filled with love. In His right hand He held what appeared to be seven small stars, spheres of burning, white-hot, incandescent matter.

I fell at His feet as though I were a dead man. I was utterly overwhelmed. I buried my face in the dusty floor of the cave. He laid His hand upon my shoulder. I felt a surge of hot energy burst

*through my body. I sensed an overwhelming peace enveloping me.
I have never before felt such love!*

*"Do not be afraid John, my dear John, the one whom I love," He
said to me. "I am the first and the last, and the living One; and I
was dead, and behold, I am alive forevermore, and I hold the keys
of death and of Hades." Then He lifted my head and smiled at me. I
burst into sobs of joy as He tightened His loving grip on my shoulder.*

*"Write therefore the things which you will see," He continued, "and
the things which are, and the things which shall take place after these
things. As for the mystery of the seven stars, which you saw in My right
hand, and the seven golden lampstands: the seven stars are the angels
of the seven churches, and the seven lampstands are the seven churches."*

*At once I was in the Spirit. I felt transported. Exactly how,
I know not. But I can tell you where! I stepped through a thin,
billowing veil of earthly atmosphere—as though it were a mere
curtain—blown open by the breath of God Himself. The scenery of
this worldly life around me simply rolled back like a scroll—and
I stepped through it and away from it. I was in another world . . .
yet only one mere step from the world I had just left. I was in this
perfect place in the twinkling of an eye, and I was once again enveloped in light-bathed, irresistible love. There is nothing like it in this
earthly existence!*

*Our brother Paul was right! Truly he, too, just as he told us,
was caught up to Paradise—the third heaven! The mind cannot
comprehend the glory of that place! The ear has never heard the
sounds that I heard! I have no words other than these with which
to describe the matter.*

*I do not have time in this letter to relate all that I experienced.
What I was ordered to write, I have written in the scroll, which
you now possess. The seven letters that accompany this scroll must
be delivered at your earliest possible convenience to the respective
churches. This is an important task. I know not how the thing will
be accomplished on your part, but I am certain that it will be done
under your watch. Our Lord has commanded it.*

*Matthias, I have seen the future! I have been in the throne room
of God! I am utterly overwhelmed by what I have experienced. It was
not a dream—it was not even a mere vision. I was there! I breathed
its air! I felt its tranquility! I smelled its aromas, saw its indescribable
colors. And I spoke with angelic beings!*

I have done my best, with the simple earthly words that I possess, to describe what I have seen. In some cases I was given words and names; I felt as though they might have been clues given by our Lord for a future generation. In other cases I was simply allowed to see the scenes before my eyes, and I was told to write.

The Scroll of the Ages was opened in my presence! I saw magnificent things! I saw machines of war that could crush the Roman legions as though they were mere ants! Some of the machines (though they looked like living things!) crawled along the ground. Others flew through the air as locusts! And they contained men within them! Yet the men were unharmed; it was as though the men were riding in the bellies of these ironclad locusts! Fire issued forth from their mouths and their tails. They proved to be of great torment to the throngs that challenged them. It's all in the scroll. You will understand as the Spirit of God gives you wisdom. And so will the generations that follow.

I saw a mountain of fire rising out of the sea! I saw stars falling from the heavens, and demonic forces bearing down upon the earth like a vise. I saw a thousand streams of fiery hell gushing from the earth! Men were in torment because of the opening of the Abyss.

I saw the abomination that causes desolation! It will soon stand in the Holy Place, Matthias! It is an unspeakable horror. Domitian is a foreshadowing of the Antichrist; this I now know. But he is not the one of whom our Jesus spoke. There is one who will come—in the very last days. I have seen him. I beheld his face but was prohibited from publishing a detailed description. He will make our Domitian seem like a benevolent father!

I saw the end of days. I saw the Great Throne of Judgment. I saw the new heaven and the new earth! I saw it all! I speak the truth.

Forgive my rambling, Matthias. Please be faithful in your handling and the delivery of this material. We are conveying the words of God for many generations to come. It is a task that has engulfed me with its enormity. I pray that God will help me to fully accomplish it.

Prochorus sends his greetings. He is well. Pray for us. Give my greetings and my love to the saints. May the Lord bless you and keep you forever.

—JOHN[1]

2

I REMEMBER

Nothing is ever really lost to us as long as we remember it.
—L. M. MONTGOMERY, *The Story Girl*

I remember the beginning of the Gulf War, in January 1991, as if it were yesterday.

I was thirty-five at the time. With Saddam Hussein's invasion of Kuwait, regardless of one's religious persuasion in those days, there seemed to be consensus awareness that something deeply spiritual might be stirring in the world. People who had not set foot in a church in many years suddenly drifted toward worship services—and some, toward pastoral counseling. Numerous churches swelled to capacity crowds.

There was something about Saddam Hussein—with his abject

butchery, blasphemous declarations, and continual barrage of threats of producing the mother of all battles—that felt absolutely supernatural. Almost everybody commented on that fact. I remember it well.

CNN, the world's first twenty-four-hour news channel, barely over a decade old at the time, was covering the United States' response to the Kuwait invasion *live*—the first such as-it-happened war coverage in television history. The United States, and twenty-seven coalition allies, launched their offensive against Saddam Hussein and his Iraqi forces on a Wednesday evening. The date was January 16, 1991. Operation Desert Storm was under way.

The next day, in retaliation for the coalition invasion, Iraq horrified the world by launching eight Scud missiles into Israel. On that same day, Jeffrey Zaun was America's first fighter pilot to be downed in that war. The emotions of the American public were on edge.

On Friday of that first week of the war, Iraq unleashed more Scud attacks on Israel. Evening news anchors breathlessly reported that at least some of the Scuds might have contained warheads with payloads of chemical weapons. Saddam was known as a chemical weapons mass murderer—having, in the recent past, unleashed the dreaded armament upon his own people.

In the midst of the frenzy, the United States implored Israel to exercise restraint. Israeli citizens dutifully donned their government-issued gas masks and huddled in their bomb shelters. With twenty-four-hour cable news coverage, the horrified world watched together and held its collective breath.

By November 1990, the United States military had amassed more than 200,000 troops in Saudi Arabia—and even more piled into the Middle East over the next two months.

Just a few months earlier, in August 1990, Iraqi dictator-madman Saddam Hussein had launched a massive five-month attack on its tiny oil-rich neighbor, Kuwait. As U.S. troops gathered in the Middle East and coalition forces were being built by the George H. W. Bush administration in Washington, D.C., newscasters predicted a horrifyingly high number of American military casualties. Some analysts estimated that U.S. troop loss could go into the multiplied thousands if we actually engaged Iraq in the dreaded but seemingly unavoidable war. Prayers—and political maneuvering—intensified.

In the months leading up to the Gulf War, and especially in the first hours of the actual engagement, people around the globe asked: *Does this looming war have any biblical significance? Could this be the beginning of a soon-coming World War III?*

I told my congregants that, although I was unprepared to make a definitive statement on its particular biblical place, I could only believe it must carry at least *some* degree of biblical importance. Hundreds of thousands of troops from a huge, multinational coalition were gathering in the area of the famed and biblical Euphrates River. Several biblical passages actually predict an end-time war in that precise location.

The Muslim world was being stirred into frenzy in an unprecedented manner. The entire Middle East was on high alert. All the while, more Iraqi-launched Scud missiles began to rain down upon Israel, and the Israelis were prepared to exercise their powerful and legendary Samson Option, if need be.[1] Additionally, there was tremendous anxiety among Muslims, the world over, about America stationing its troops on Saudi soil. To some, especially radical Islamists, this move was nothing short of a blasphemous outrage. Threats of eventual retaliation ensued.

Over the next several days, the coalition forces, undeniably led and directed by US forces, launched an unprecedented and technologically advanced military fury upon the Iraqi military and its famed Republican Guard. On February 25, 1991, in retaliation, Iraqi forces fired a Scud missile at an American barracks in Dhahran, Saudi Arabia. The attack killed twenty-eight US military personnel. The United States and coalition forces continued to unleash their ferocity.

On February 26, the demoralized Iraqi troops began retreating from Kuwait, but only after they had set eight hundred of the tiny Gulf state's oil wells on fire—in retribution. The hellish plumes of blazing fire and sooty-black smoke billowed into the air and boiled across the desert. The spectacle was reminiscent of a scene straight out of a horror movie. We watched it live on television. For many, the unfolding drama had an end-of-the-world feel to it. With all its technology, even Hollywood could not have produced such an awe-inspiring and spectacular scene.

However, a mere one hundred hours after the war had started—a ceasefire was called and President George H. W. Bush declared Kuwait to be liberated. The war was over in fewer than five days; the Iraqi military had been decimated. The major highway coming out of Kuwait had earned the nickname "the Highway of Death" because of the havoc and carnage leveled against the retreating, brutally humiliated Iraqi troops.

Of Iraq's 545,000 troops in the Kuwait theater of operations, an estimated 100,000 were killed, and 300,000 were wounded. The American battle statistics were much less dramatic—148 U.S. battle deaths, and 145 non-battle deaths, including 15 women. The total of those wounded in action was 467.[2]

America was euphoric. Predictably, church attendance eventually began to dwindle. After all, God had answered the world's collective prayers—it was time to get back to *normal* life. We apparently did not need supernatural intervention any longer. We had just witnessed the unanswerable and unstoppable military might of the world's greatest superpower and its coalition allies. Sure, there would be months, perhaps even years, of troops on the ground and no-fly zones, nation rebuilding, and the like—but we had won; life was good again.

Still, I could not shake the feeling, deep inside my soul, that what the world had just witnessed was only the beginning of even more horrendous things to come. I was certain of it. I remember those days well. If we had only known what was yet to come. If we had only known that, perhaps, it had just begun.

3
COULD IT BE?

Coincidence is God's way of remaining anonymous.

—ALBERT EINSTEIN, *The World as I See It*

Is it possible that World Wars I and II; the miraculous rebirth of the nation of Israel; the Chernobyl nuclear disaster; the Iraqi invasion of Kuwait; the subsequent Gulf War; the terrorist attacks of 9/11 in New York City and Washington, D.C.; the Iraq and Afghanistan Wars; the Arab Spring Muslim uprisings of the Middle East; and the continual alignment of Muslim nations who desire to wipe Israel off the face of the map are specifically related? Countless students of the Word of God claim that they are. However, is there actually reliable documentation that leads to this conclusion? And even if the conclusion is correct, could not the threads of these seeming associations be mere coincidence?

Is it also possible, as some are now reporting, that the majority of the aforementioned events are foretold in the Bible? And could it be that most of them were foretold through coded or key words contained within certain biblical prophecies?

Furthermore, is it reasonable to believe that several of the events are actually keyed into the visions of the renowned seven trumpets found in the New Testament book of Revelation, those famous apocalyptic images given to the apostle John on the island of Patmos more than two thousand years ago? Could it really be possible that, with the Bible in one hand and the headline news of our generation in the other, we are watching biblical end-time prophecy unfold before the eyes of the world?

Numerous Bible students, after meticulously poring over these specific words of biblical prophecy and comparing them to monumental events of world history, believe the answer to each of these questions is an extremely plausible "Yes!"

> "As I read the news, I can't help but wonder if we are in the last hours before our Lord Jesus Christ returns to rescue His church and God pours out His wrath on the world for the rejection of His Son."
>
> —FRANKLIN GRAHAM, *September 4, 2014*[1]

You will soon have the opportunity to make an informed decision for yourself.

IS GOD PEEKING AT US THROUGH THE CURTAINS?

We live in a world in which humanistic "science" has attempted to convince us, for well over a hundred years, that there is no Grand Designer. Everything is here, they declare, as a result of a cosmic accident and unplanned, unreasoned, and relatively random evolutionary processes. However, while at the same time that certain Bible prophecies seem to be literally exploding off the pages within our historical lifetime, science is also running into some amazing and unexplainable conundrums. Some of these scientific roadblocks seem to suggest that there actually is incredibly little happenstance involved in the mechanics of the world around us. Surprise, surprise! Consider this example from a leading evolutionary scientist. Dr. Paul Charles William Davies is a British-born physicist, writer, and broadcaster. He is currently a professor at Arizona State University as well as the director of BEYOND: Center for Fundamental Concepts in Science.

The focus of Dr. Davies's research is in the fields of cosmology, quantum field theory, and astrobiology. In 2005, he took up the chair of the SETI: Post-Detection Science and Technology Taskgroup of the International Academy of Astronautics. Observe Dr. Davies's words, written in 2007, concerning the areas of supposed coincidence within the physical world:

> Scientists are slowly waking up to an inconvenient truth—the universe looks suspiciously like a fix. The issue concerns the very laws of nature themselves. For 40 years, physicists and cosmologists have been quietly collecting examples of all too convenient "coincidences" and special features in the underlying laws of the universe that seem to be necessary in order for life, and hence conscious beings, to exist. Change any one of them and the consequences would be lethal. Fred Hoyle, the distinguished cosmologist, once said it was as if "a super-intellect has monkeyed with physics."
>
> To see the problem, imagine playing God with the cosmos. Before you is a designer machine that lets you tinker with the basics of physics. Twiddle this knob and you make all electrons a bit lighter, twiddle that one and you make gravity a bit stronger, and so on. It happens that you need to set thirty something knobs to fully describe the world about us. The crucial point is that some of those metaphorical knobs must be tuned very precisely, or the universe would be sterile.[2]

While admiring Dr. Davies's scientific candor, it is amazing to observe the conclusion to which he ultimately arrives. And while he is clear in the rest of his material that he does not believe in the necessity of the existence of God, he admits there is a law-like order to the universe. He further attests that this undeniable order is an inconvenient truth for evolutionary-minded scientists. He admits (in so many words) that the logical conclusion one should reach is that a design demands the presence of a designer. Which brings me back to the point of this brief chapter: If there is an eternally existing, sovereign, and omniscient God who designed the universe and is directing it toward its sovereignly predetermined conclusion, why should we be surprised that He has left those who are His children some clues to the *beginning* of that encoded conclusion?

Should it surprise us to discover that, in the written Word of the sovereign Creator of the universe, there might be keys to monumental events—events that, when tied together, direct a specific generation to the fact that they are living in the times just before the Lord's return?

It could well be that we are living in the trumpet days of Revelation. These unbelievably connected and unprecedented events may be the fulfillment of biblical prophecy meant specifically for our generation, given to us by the God who is directing the entire story. Read on. You may never again look at the Bible, or the evening news, in the same way.

4

TO RAPTURE OR *NOT* TO RAPTURE—
THAT IS THE QUESTION

I spent a lot of time thinking about contemporary Christianity, and obviously the rapture kept coming up . . . My first impulse was . . . to laugh it off—it's sort of a funny idea, people just floating away. But I kept thinking: What if it did happen? . . . I thought, I'm such a skeptic that even if it did happen, I would resist the implications of it, and I also thought that three years later, everyone would have forgotten about it. No matter what horrible thing happens in the world, the culture seems to move on.

—TOM PERROTTA, *New York Times* bestselling author[1]

The topic of the specific timing of the rapture should not be a fellowship-dividing subject.

While the timing of the rapture certainly is an important matter of consideration, in my estimation, it simply cannot be the most important theological concern, primarily because the Bible does not unequivocally state exactly when the rapture of the church will occur. The fact that so many sincere and biblically literate people of high academic standing cannot agree on this important matter is prima facie evidence that the Bible is not crystal clear regarding a precision-outlined timeline.

Few people state the matter any better than Dr. David Reagan. Dr. Reagan is founder and president of Lamb & Lion Ministries and host of Christ in Prophecy television. His ministry and television programming reach into the homes of millions of people around the world. He has been preaching and teaching the Word of God and conducting national and international prophecy conferences for forty years. I consider him a dear friend.

Dr. Reagan believes strongly in a pre-tribulation view of the rapture. Although we do not agree on the matter of the rapture's possible timing, I honor him for his godly stance concerning the issue—I have adopted the spirit of his position as my own: "My final observation is that I am not dogmatic about the timing of the Rapture," he says, "[un]like some of my colleagues who are downright uncompromising about the timing . . . The Bible never clearly states when the Rapture will occur, and there is, therefore, legitimate room for differences of opinion. I believe the best inference of scripture is a Pre-Tribulation Rapture, but it is still only an inference."[2]

Another man whom I count as a good friend, Joel Richardson (*New York Times* bestselling author of *The Islamic Antichrist* and *Mideast Beast*), states the matter in a similarly elegant manner. Joel does not hold to a pre-tribulation rapture belief. On his blog, in an article titled "Rapture: Pre-trib, Post-trib, or Pre-Wrath?" Joel says:

> I've rarely written concerning the issue of the rapture. My reason for this is because of the tendency for this issue to stir up disputes, divisions, and a high level of emotion amongst the brethren. When I have commented on this issue, I've tried to avoid emphasizing the timing issue, and more so emphasize the applicational, pastoral aspect of the discussion. Is the view that we hold causing us to have a deep sense of urgency for evangelism, missions, and the pursuit of holiness, etc.? Are we preparing ourselves, and those who listen to us, to face antichrists and great tribulation?[3]

And many share Joel's concern that we must, first and foremost, prepare the church for tough days ahead. We must equip the church to be witnesses of Jesus Christ even in the most difficult of days that may potentially lie just ahead.

Can we not agree that to stand dogmatically upon a singular position in a matter such as this, not directly settled by the Scriptures themselves, to the point of breaking fellowship with a fellow believer, borders on the error of the ancient Pharisees? After all, the Pharisees were the ones who claimed to have had the *best* knowledge of the Word of God concerning the coming of the long-awaited Messiah. Yet, when the Messiah *did* come, fulfilling all the appropriate messianic prophecies, they completely missed Him! And they did not miss Him by *just a little*—they missed Him *by a mile*!

As a matter of fact, in the name of God, under the auspices of doing the holy work of God, within a stone's throw of the temple of God, the ancient Pharisees actually arranged for the crucifixion of the Son of God. And the whole time they truly thought they were doing God a favor! Even though the Pharisees fervently insisted they knew *the truth* concerning the Messiah and His coming, they were wrong—*fervently* wrong.

We can be certain that the Lord obviously knows the exact timing of the rapture and *every* other end-time event. He is the one who has set them all in motion. Accordingly, I believe He has given us clues in His Word so that we may discern the times in which we live. That is one of the reasons His prophetic Word was given. He has not left His children in the dark. However, the most essential thing for us to know is that Jesus *is coming* for His church and that He *will* return to rule and reign in righteousness after He pours out His final wrath on an unbelieving generation. To this great and settled biblical truth I say, with John the Revelator, "Even so, come, Lord Jesus, come!"

Let me clearly state my eschatological leanings: I do not hold to a pre-tribulation view of the rapture. Regardless of the exact timing of the rapture, I certainly believe it will occur *before* the wrath of God is finally unleashed. That is to say (without boring you with all the many theological details and debates), I believe the rapture of the church will occur sometime *after* the Antichrist is revealed and the *Tribulation* (generally believed to be a period of seven years) of the last days begins. But, while holding this interpretation, I also make two qualifying statements:

1. I hope I am mistaken. I would love for it to be that the church is raptured *before* the appearance of the Antichrist and *before* the Great Tribulation takes place. However, I simply have not yet been able to contextually reconcile the Scriptures to this viewpoint. That does not mean that I am right and the pre-tribulation rapture crowd is wrong—it simply means that I do not see it that way . . . yet.

2. I leave myself room to grow, room to learn, and room to be mistaken in any area of eschatology. I have learned over my many years of study and preaching that I desperately do not want to make the tragic pharisaical mistake of insisting that I *am* right because I *have* to be right. However, I do *want* to be right, in as much as is possible, when it comes to the accurate handling of the Word of God.

This understanding of eschatology, by the way, is certainly not outside the boundaries of a mainstream theological view. Consider Dr. Herschel Hobbs, a former two-term president of the Southern Baptist Convention.

Dr. Hobbs was the vice president of the Baptist World Alliance for five years. He pastored the First Baptist Church in Oklahoma City from 1949 to 1972 and is best known for having served as the chairman of the committee that wrote the statement of Southern Baptist doctrine, "The Baptist Faith and Message." He was a prolific author, and for many years his sermons and doctrinal messages were broadcast over hundreds of radio programs around the United States. Educated at Howard College and Southern Theological Seminary, Dr. Hobbs held a bachelor's, a master's, and a doctorate in theology, and a doctor of divinity degree. When he died, he was revered throughout the nation, so much so the *New York Times* ran a special story about his life, his ministry, and his theological achievements.[4]

In his book *The Fundamentals of Our Faith*, Dr. Hobbs includes the following explanation of the rapture's timing in the chapter titled "Eschatology or Last Things":

> The tribulation is to last seven years, after which Christ will return in power and glory. Let us note, however, that Jesus presents the rapture as coming after the tribulation (Matthew 24:29–31). The word "tribulation" both in Hebrew and Greek means distress, pressure, or affliction. It is connected with the idea of persecution. In Matthew 24:21 Jesus spoke of suffering connected with the destruction of Jerusalem. To his disciples he said, "in the world ye shall have tribulation (John 16:33)." It is to this later end that Jesus refers in Matthew 24:29. "Immediately after the tribulation of those days shall the sun be darkened." It would seem that tribulation refers not to a post-rapture persecution of the Jews [as in the pre-rapture postulation] but to the sufferings endured by Christ's followers throughout Christian history (Matthew 24:8–14).
>
> That the tribulation refers to the experience of Christians in proclaiming the gospel is clearly seen in Revelation 1:9, 2:9–10, 22; 7:14. In this light, therefore, it would seem that we can best understand Matthew 24:29–31. The rapture of the saints [the Church] comes at the end of the tribulation of the saints.[5]

I am not quoting Dr. Hobbs because I consider his view to be the infallible and final word on this controversial matter, although Dr. Hobbs was certainly not alone among a plethora of other highly respected biblical scholars that held, and currently hold, this same view of eschatology. Rather, I am quoting his view as one example of many, so a reader who may be relatively new to the differing views of the rapture's timing will not consider my view a "strange teaching" or an "unbiblical doctrine."

Now, let us turn to a brief study of what the Bible actually says about that grand event of joyous expectation that Christians know as the *rapture*.

5

THE FACT OF THE RAPTURE

WARNING: In case of Rapture, this car will be unmanned.

—popular bumper sticker

Before 1948, many deeply respected commentators and prophecy experts declared that the biblically prophesied return of Israel to the land, as a recognized nation of the world, would not happen before the literal return of Jesus Christ. In fact, many such experts proclaimed the event could not happen until the return of Jesus—simply because the rebirth of a *real Israel* was a human impossibility. Some scholars even suggested that the return of Israel was clearly figurative and was to be taken only in a spiritual sense.

A literal return of Israel was unthinkable. After all, Israel had been gone from the land for well over two thousand years. The Jews were scattered over the face of the earth. No nation in history, thus destroyed and scattered, had ever returned to its status as a premier nation. The prevailing Middle East politics would have made it impossible for any such event to occur. How could a long-dead nation be restored to the locale of its original territory, speaking its original language, observing many of its original customs, and situated in such a precarious geopolitical condition, all the while in a place of power and prominence such as described in the Bible? It was an utter impossibility . . . so they thought.

However, every one of the scholars—read those words again—*every one of them* who held such a view was mistaken. Even the most highly respected among the commentators was wrong. The prophecy experts who wrote scholarly books and were the most sought after for conferences—their teaching was faulty too. That is an amazing and humbling fact to consider.

For Israel *did* return to the land (in Ezekiel 37 fashion), and they *are* speaking their original language, they *are* observing many of their original customs, and they *are* a world force and power with which to be reckoned. In addition, Israel has been at the center of the evening news practically every week since its rebirth!

Most of the Middle East negotiations, wars, and geopolitical rumblings of today are a direct result of Israel's returned and revived presence in the land of Palestine. Furthermore, the coalition of enemy nations desiring to destroy a returned Israel (spoken of in Ezekiel 38 and Psalm 83, for example) is drafting up its destructive plans for Israel right before our eyes and ears.

Those who are particularly certain the rapture of the church will occur *before* the tribulation period will often argue that for Christ to return, or for the rapture to occur, *nothing* else needs to happen in the way of specific events. For example, years ago they would have said that it was not necessary for Israel to return to the land, nor is it necessary for the world to see the Antichrist first, and so forth.

The fact of the matter is that Israel *did* return to the land, and the rapture has not yet occurred. Therefore, to be biblically correct in the matter, the return of Israel to the land *was* a last-days sign that *had* to occur before the rapture of the church and the return of Jesus Christ. This is no small point of consideration and distinctly proves there may be more biblical conditions that must yet be fulfilled before the church is raptured.

Some counter this position by claiming the nation of Israel, which now exists in the Middle East, is not the *real* Israel. They claim it is a *fake* Israel. But the fallacy of this claim is that nowhere in the Bible does it even hint there will be a fake Israel in the last days. However, there is a plethora of scriptures pointing to the literal return of a geographical Israel. Those prophecies actually begin in the book of Deuteronomy, and this was *before* the Israelis had even set foot in the Promised Land for the first time!

> The LORD will scatter you among the peoples, and only a few of you will survive among the nations to which the LORD will drive you. . . .
> Then the LORD your God will restore your fortunes and have compassion on you and gather you again from all the nations where he scattered you. Even if you have been banished to the most distant land under the heavens, from there the LORD your God will gather you and bring you back. He will bring you to the land that belonged to your fathers, and you will take possession of it. He will make you more prosperous and numerous than your fathers.
> —DEUT. 4:27; 30:3–5 NIV

And Israel is there . . . back in the land. And there has been no rapture yet. The rapture *is* coming. But it did not come *before* Israel came back to the land and dominated the attention of the world . . . just as the Bible contextually predicted. My cautious position in interpreting prophecy and eschatology does not come from a desire to "walk the fence" or play games with the people of God. My cautiousness comes from a common-sense and—hopefully—humble understanding that until certain end-time prophecies actually unfold in their completeness before the eyes of the world, we would be foolish to dogmatically declare that we *know* with certainty what every one of these prophecies means and *exactly* how they will be represented.

The Pharisees (the best Bible scholars on the planet in their day) got it wrong in the time of Jesus. Numerous commentators and experts before 1948 got it wrong in their day. Is it possible that some modern-day teachers of prophecy might be getting at least a few important things wrong today by insisting that they know exactly how end-time events *must* unfold?

THE WORD *RAPTURE* IS NOT IN THE BIBLE?

There can be no serious denial that the Bible teaches there will be an eventual rapture event. Yet, there is an entire movement afoot in the Christian subculture that says there will be no rapture . . . at all. However, in context, the Scripture simply does not support that proposition. The only thing that serious students of the rapture topic have much debate about is—will it come before, during, or after the Great Tribulation period? Since the rapture occurrence, therefore, appears to be a biblical certainty, it seems the biggest point of debate that remains is the timetable.

It is a fact that the particular word *rapture* is not found in the Bible. At least, it is not found in the English Bible, or the original Greek in which the New Testament was written. However, the concept of the rapture is clearly presented in the Word of God.

The word *rapture*, or *raeptius* (Latin), is in the Vulgate. The Vulgate is the Latin-language version of the Bible, produced by theology scholar Jerome in the early AD 400s. Pope Damasus I commissioned the work in AD 382. It was Jerome who gave the Latin designation *rapture* to the original Greek verb *harpázō* (#726 in *Strong's Greek Dictionary*), defined simply as being "seized." Observe the words of the apostle Paul in this matter: "For the Lord himself shall descend from heaven with a shout, with the voice of the archangel, and with the trump of God: and the dead in Christ shall rise first: Then we which are alive and remain shall be *caught up* [harpazo] together with them *in the clouds,* to meet the Lord *in the air:* and so shall we ever be with the Lord. Wherefore comfort one another with these words" (1 Thess. 4:16–18; emphasis added). Notice how Paul's description of the rapture includes the sounding of a trumpet.

It is also a fact that Jesus spoke of a "gathering together" of his "elect" (the church) at his return. Observe Jesus' use of the word *trumpet* as well, in association with this end-time gathering, or rapture: "And then shall appear the sign of the Son of man in heaven: and then shall all the tribes of the earth mourn, and they shall see the Son of man coming in the clouds of heaven with power and great glory. And he shall send his angels with a great *sound of a trumpet,* and they *shall gather together* his elect from the four winds, from one end of heaven to the other" (Matt. 24:30–31; emphasis added).

The English words *gather together* are the operative words in this passage. In the Greek, the singular word representing the English concept of gathering together is *episynágō,* which means "to collect upon the same place" (*Strong's* #1996).

After reading the words of Jesus and Paul, it is difficult to contextually deny the fact of the rapture. Sometime in the last days, God's people will be gathered together in one place while being seized up and away—taken out of the way—*raptured.* This rapture event prepares the way for the outpouring of God's wrath. We know this with certainty because the children of God, though they may (in my view) undergo a certain amount of tribulation (even great tribulation), will not be subjected to God's terrible wrath. That unmitigated and holy fury is reserved only for those who have spurned and rejected the glory and mercy of God by rejecting Jesus Christ as Lord and Savior.

> But let us, who are of the day, be sober, putting on the breastplate of faith and love; and for an helmet, the hope of salvation.

For God hath not appointed us to wrath, but to obtain salvation by
our Lord Jesus Christ, who died for us, that, whether we wake
or sleep, we should live together with him.
—1 THESS. 5:8–10; *emphasis added*

Since it appears to be a biblically settled matter that God's
people will *not* undergo His wrath, it would be beneficial for us to
be aware of the difference between the concepts of *tribulation* and
God's wrath. Defining these terms within their proper context is
important in correctly understanding end-time prophecy. The next
chapter will clearly set out the differences.

6

TRIBULATION OR WRATH?

Don't you remember that when I was with you I used to tell you these things?
—THE APOSTLE PAUL[1]

T o state the matter simply, tribulation is not the same thing as God's wrath. The word *tribulation* means "trouble or distress." Not only did Jesus tell His disciples, "In this world you will have tribulation" (John 16:33), but He also gave us ample instructions concerning how to live in the *midst* of tribulation. God's people have always endured persecution—sometimes severe, unbearable, and unthinkable persecution. Tribulation is brought upon the people of God by a sinful, godless, and spiritually decaying world system. Who are we to declare the church will not go through tribulation? Many believe it certainly would be a difficult thing to try and persuade our Christian brothers and sisters living in decidedly anti-Christian nations that they will not endure any type of great tribulation. Given the fact that many of them are already experiencing excessive fines, their property and assets being seized, and even torture and death, they might ask us, "How can tribulation be any greater than this?"

To be fair, those who would take issue with this question often respond with one, or all, of the following three statements:

1. There is a big difference between *regular* tribulation and the days of the ultimate *Great* Tribulation.

My response: Yes, but how do we measure tribulation by degrees when it is your family that is being imprisoned, beaten, maimed, raped, tortured, executed? It is an amazingly comfortable and convenient thing to be living in a relatively persecution-free society, proclaiming that God's people (the church) will not have to experience real tribulation. Yet, more Christians were killed for their faith in the twentieth century alone than have been martyred in the total history of Christianity.[2] A 2010 report from the Catholic organization Aid to the Church in Need revealed that at least 75 percent of the religious persecution reported around the world from 2008 to 2010 was directed at Christians.[3] Therefore, Jesus' words in Matthew 24:21 are already true: "For then shall be great tribulation, such as was not since the beginning of the world to this time, no, nor ever shall be"!

2. Well then, you must believe that God is a wife beater!

My response: The implication of the accusation is that if Jesus does not return for His bride *before* the Tribulation—then we must believe that He condones and allows the abuse of His bride. However, the argument neglects the truth that tribulation is brought upon God's people by a sinful world, not by His own hand. Persecution against the church has been present in every generation—even terrible, unthinkable persecution. Do you remember reading about the days of the Roman emperors and, also, the Inquisition? And, according to my understanding of the Scriptures, it is precisely because the Antichrist is so mercilessly persecuting the bride of Christ during the Great Tribulation that Jesus *does* return, to rescue His abused bride from the hands of the evil world system. The *world* is abusing the bride—not Jesus. Jesus is the Knight in shining armor who comes to rescue the bride in the last days.

3. Oh . . . so you don't believe in the imminent rapture of the church? You are looking for the Antichrist *before* you are looking for Jesus!

My response: We *do* hope for, long for, and pray for the rapture of the church to happen—today! Hardly a day goes by that many of us do not pray in some way, "Even so, come, Lord Jesus, come!" However, if our understanding is correct, then there *will* be things that happen in the world just before the rapture of the church. We simply want to be watchful and ready, according to what we believe the Bible teaches in this matter. By the way— many Bible students believe they see strong scriptural support for the notion that the Antichrist will make his appearance on the world scene before God's people are gathered to Him in the rapture. For instance:

Concerning the coming of our Lord Jesus Christ *and our being gathered to him* [raptured], we ask you, brothers, not to become easily unsettled or alarmed by the teaching allegedly by us—whether by a prophecy or by word of mouth or by letter— asserting that the day of the Lord has already come. Don't let anyone deceive you in any way, for that day *will not come until the rebellion occurs and the man of lawlessness is revealed*, the man doomed to destruction. He will oppose and will exalt himself over everything that is called God or is worshiped, so that he sets himself up in God's temple, proclaiming himself to be God. Don't you remember that when I was with you I used to tell you these things?

—2 THESS. 2:1–5 NIV, *emphasis added*

Interestingly, Paul declared that he had made this fact crystal clear in his previous preaching at the church in Thessalonica. Unfortunately, false teachers had slipped in among them and brought them to a point of confusion in the matter. However, the main position Paul wished to emphasize was that the gathering together of God's people (specific rapture language is used here) will not occur before the Antichrist's appearance.

THE WRATH OF GOD

God's wrath is an altogether different consideration. The wrath of the Lord is the specific and directed anger of God, poured out on the unbelieving world system. It is this wicked antichrist system that will be involved in persecuting His children in the last days. The wrath of God is a dreadful, unimaginable, unequaled, and terrifying thing—ask Pharaoh of Moses' day. Ask the people of Sodom and Gomorrah. Ask the people of Noah's generation!

The Bible is clear—God will pour out His unmitigated wrath on those who are left behind after the bride of Christ (the church) has been taken out of the way (raptured).

Let me introduce an illustration that will clearly demonstrate the difference between tribulation and wrath. Consider this scenario:

You have dropped your precious wife off at a community event. It is an event where she has important business to attend to, and you were happy to accommodate her.

Much later in the evening, at the time of your return, as you pull into the parking lot, you observe your wife being accosted by a couple of thugs. They are slapping her around—one has just knocked her to the ground. She is screaming for her life. She is not even aware that you are on the premises yet. And neither are the thugs. However, you *are* there. You *do* see what is happening. And you just happen to have a Louisville Slugger behind the seat of your car.

I think you get the picture from there. (I know I have a picture in my mind.)

But here is the point: Your wife is being abused at the hands of lawless men. She is being *persecuted*. But you have faithfully returned for her, just as you promised. You are there, and you see what is happening. You will not allow the abuse to occur even one moment more. You snatch (rapture) her out of the way and unleash your furious wrath upon the evildoers. Though she suffered severely, it is nothing compared to what you will do to the perpetrators of the crime against your loved one. They will suffer the full extent of your wrath. Your wife was *not* appointed to suffer your wrath—but the lawless men will surely get a taste of it. Your wife will go home with you—to your love and tender mercies. The evil men are going to jail (after a stop at the emergency room). Do you get the picture now?

"In the world ye shall have tribulation," Jesus said (John 16:33). And Paul assures us, "God hath not appointed us [His Church] to wrath." (1 Thess. 5:9)

The Old Testament bears out this same order of the last days timetable. There are clear pictures of the tribulation of God's people, the rapture of God's people, and the outpouring of God's wrath—right there, plain as day, in the Old Testament. They were recorded, I believe, as illustrations of the greater truth to come . . . the rapture of the church. Consider the following three striking illustrations:

NOAH AND THE FLOOD

In Noah's day the world was exceedingly wicked. In fact, it was so wicked that God announced He would destroy it all—every man, woman, child, and beast. In the midst of this wickedness, only Noah and his family found favor in the eyes of God. Do you really have any doubt, in the most wicked time the earth had ever seen, that God's people (Noah and his family) did not suffer tribulation, even *great* tribulation? Did God bring his wrath down upon that unbelieving world? Yes He did. He destroyed them all. But before God destroyed everything, what did He do for *His* people? He lifted them *up, above* His wrath! He raptured them out! In the ark they were saved.

The ark represents our salvation, which is found in Jesus. It also represents that certain coming of the Lord and promised rapture of God's people in the last days, just before He pours out His wrath on the unbelieving world. Consider the following:

> As it was in the days of Noah, so it will be at the coming of the Son of Man. For in the days before the flood, people were eating and drinking, marrying and giving in marriage, up to the day Noah entered the ark; and they knew nothing about what would happen until the flood came and took them all away. That is how it will be at the coming of the Son of Man.
>
> —MATT. 24:37–39 NIV

> God waited patiently in the days of Noah while the ark was being built. In it only a few people, eight in all, were saved through water, and this water symbolizes baptism that now saves you also—not the removal of dirt from the body but the pledge of a good conscience toward God. It saves you by the resurrection of Jesus Christ, who has gone into heaven and is at God's right hand—with angels, authorities and powers in submission to him.
>
> —1 PETER 3:20–22 NIV

EGYPT AND MOSES

God's people, the children of Israel, were under severe tribulation in the days of Pharaoh (a type of the Antichrist). They were being tortured, abused, and tormented daily (great tribulation). But God brought forth a deliverer named Moses. Moses took the children of Israel out of Egypt and to the edge of the Red Sea. Pharaoh's army swept down upon them in fury. However, the Red Sea was opened, and the children of God went through the wall of water (raptured) and into their journey to the Promised Land (a picture of heaven). In the meantime, God caused that same wall of water to come crashing down upon Pharaoh and his army (God's wrath), thus destroying the enemies of God's people before their eyes. The children of Israel suffered years of great tribulation in Egypt (a type of last-days wicked world system), but God's people were eventually delivered, and His terrible wrath fell on those godless ones who were left behind. The pattern is unmistakable.

SODOM AND GOMORRAH

The days of Sodom and Gomorrah were so depraved that God declared He would wipe the two cities and their people from the face of the earth. We read in Genesis 13 of the great iniquity of the Sodomites and the persecution likely endured by God's only righteous people in that area—Lot and his family. Even the New Testament records the desperately wicked times of tribulation in which Lot's family lived. Yet, God delivered them. How did He deliver them? By sending angels—who took them out, or raptured them—just before the wrath of God fell upon the cities:

> If He [God] condemned the cities of Sodom and Gomorrah by burning them to ashes, and made them an example of what is going to happen to the ungodly; and if he rescued Lot, a righteous man, who was distressed by the filthy lives of lawless men (for that righteous man, living among them day after day, was tormented in his righteous soul by the lawless deeds he saw and heard)—if this is so, then the Lord knows how to rescue godly men from trials and to hold the unrighteous for the day of judgment, while continuing their punishment.
> —2 PETER 2:6–9 NIV

Notice that Peter used the illustration of Sodom and Gomorrah's destruction to declare that in the midst of tribulation, God rescues (raptures) His children, and then brings down His wrath upon the unbelievers. This is exactly what many believe to be the correct interpretation of the rapture in the last days of our time.

Now, observe the words of Jesus concerning these matters. Jesus also used the examples of Noah's flood and the cities of Sodom and Gomorrah to illustrate the unfolding of events in the last days.

> Just as it was in the days of Noah, so also will it be in the days of the Son of Man. People were eating, drinking, marrying and being given in marriage up to the day Noah entered the ark. Then the flood came and destroyed them all. It was the same in the days of Lot. People were eating and drinking, buying and selling, planting and building. But the day Lot left Sodom, fire and sulfur rained down from heaven and destroyed them all. It will be just like this on the day the Son of Man is revealed.
>
> —LUKE 17:26–30 niv

Note that in using these illustrations, Jesus declared: "It will be just like this." And how *was* it in those days? As you have seen, God's people lived in times of great tribulation. Then, God arranged for their deliverance in the midst of that tribulation. Next, God brought down His wrath on those left behind. The pattern is unmistakable. And Jesus said it would be "just like" that again.

A FALLING AWAY?

In my estimation, there is another important reason to give serious consideration to a mid-tribulation, or post-tribulation (pre-wrath), understanding of the rapture's timing. First, as I have already demonstrated, the Bible is not dogmatically clear about the exact timing of the rapture. But second, there is a logical consideration. If the rapture does, in fact, occur before the tribulation, then all bornagain believers will be taken out and up before the appearance of the Antichrist, and even before the Great Tribulation begins.

On the other hand, by helping believers see the possibility of the body of Christ experiencing a certain amount of tribulation and persecution just before the rapture of the church and the return of Jesus Christ, we may be performing a great service to the family of believers.

At least two times in the book of Revelation John warned the saints that the tribulation will require patience, endurance, and faithfulness (see Revelation 13:10 and 14:12). This is an important warning. Exactly who are the *saints* of God? The word *saint* simply means "separated one." How is one separated unto God—especially in the New Testament days, in which, and for which, the book of Revelation was written? The only ones who are truly separated unto God are those who are bought by the blood of Jesus Christ—in other words, born-again believers (Jew or Gentile), what we call Christians or "followers of Christ."

Accordingly, it would appear that Christians are specifically warned of the persecution they will suffer at the hands of the Antichrist in the last days just *before* the rapture of the church. There are those who say these "saints" are those who were saved after the rapture. Some even claim that these are Jews who were saved after the rapture of the church. These are interesting conjectures, but the Bible does not plainly declare either of these things.

If I am wrong in the final analysis, then there has been no great harm done—I was simply wrong, and we *are* raptured before the appearance of the Antichrist and before the Great Tribulation. But if I am right, then I want to prepare the church for some potentially tough days ahead—because many believe it could well be that we are now living in the trumpet days of Revelation.

7

UNPRECEDENTED

As human beings, we are vulnerable to confusing the unprecedented with the improbable. In our everyday experience, if something has never happened before, we are generally safe in assuming it is not going to happen in the future, but the exceptions can kill you.

—AL GORE

Life is filled with unprecedented events, most of which are trumped by an eventual duplicate or enhancement of that first event. However, there are those "unprecedented" events that have yet to be repeated or equaled. Or, if they are repeated, the multiple events are clearly associated in some conspicuous way. An example of this would be World War I and World War II. Both events were unprecedented in many ways, yet undeniably connected by historical and geopolitical circumstances.

But what if that unprecedented, worldwide event was actually foretold thousands of years before it happened? In that case, we could call that a *prophetic* happening. Consider the following catalog of events—every one of them has occurred within the last one hundred years. The majority of them have happened within the last thirty years, as of this writing. And *all* of them are connected by the fact that not only are they unprecedented, but many believe they are links in a distinctive chain of historical—and biblically prophetic—events:

WORLD WAR I

The First World War (1914–1918) was also called World War I, or *the Great War.* It is widely reported as the fifth deadliest war in history.[1] However, World War I has also been labeled unprecedented in the total amount of carnage and destruction it caused.[2] World War I was the first global war in history. It involved 65 million troops from thirty countries and claimed between 9 and 13 million lives.[3] With this designation, it was clearly an unprecedented event of global proportion. Nothing like it had ever happened before, and in fact, the only thing remotely like it grew directly *out* of it: World War II.

WORLD WAR II

World War II, or the Second World War (1939–1945), was also unprecedented in several notable ways. It was the most widespread war in history, with more than 100 million people, from well over thirty different countries of major participation (almost seventy nations were involved in one way or another) serving in military units.[4] Marked by mass deaths of civilians, including the Holocaust and the first and only use of nuclear weapons in warfare, it resulted in an estimated 50 to 85 million fatalities. This amazing wartime death toll made World War II the deadliest conflict in history.[5] Practically every nation of the world, with the exception of nine or ten neutral countries, played some role in this war of global proportion.[6] One of the most prominent results of World War II was the unprecedented mobilization and deployment of American military forces around the world. Several of the most notable and unique results of World War II were also of a distinctly biblical nature.

THE CHERNOBYL NUCLEAR DISASTER

The 1986 Chernobyl disaster was the worst nuclear accident in history, releasing an unparalleled amount of nuclear radiation into the atmosphere.[7] Unknown to many, the Chernobyl catastrophe continues to have global consequences.

The Fukushima, Japan, nuclear disaster on March 11, 2011, was also tragic. As with Chernobyl, its specific long-term effects are still unknown. However, as devastating as Fukushima was, Chernobyl initially released ten times that amount of radiation into the atmosphere.[8] As of this writing, Fukushima has not yet come close to the magnitude of disaster as the unprecedented Chernobyl catastrophe. And as you will learn later, Chernobyl continues to threaten the world with even more massive radiation expulsion. Interestingly, the technology to produce a nuclear power plant in the first place is a direct result of the nuclear technology developed in connection with World War II.

THE GULF WAR AND THE SUBSEQUENT FALLOUT

The Gulf War, or Operation Desert Storm (August 1990 to February 1991), was the mother of all unprecedented occurrences. Practically every news report covering the event used the word *unprecedented* to describe various aspects of the conflict—from the initial invasion of Kuwait by Saddam Hussein's Iraqi troops to the response by the United States and the massive multinational coalition that formed against Iraq. Consequently, many believe the Gulf War "[led] to further confrontations—and its reverberations are still felt today. Most obviously, it helped set the stage for the U.S.-led invasion of Iraq in 2003. It also became a cause celebre for Osama bin Laden and one of the factors that led to al-Qaida's attacks against the U.S. on Sept. 11, 2001."[9]

Following 9/11, the 2003 Iraq and Afghanistan wars ensued, resulting in the final toppling of the regime of Saddam Hussein, his death sentence, and the continuing war in Afghanistan.

Additionally, the *New York Times* reported that the subsequent Iraq War of 2003 was actually the true beginning of the infamous Arab Spring uprisings all over the Middle East.[10] If this is true—one can clearly see the connected chain reaction initiated by the Gulf War:

- Unprecedented and purposed destruction of hundreds of oil wells and massive oil supplies[11]

- unprecedented ecological and health disasters[12]

- unprecedented American military operations (a decidedly and crushingly victorious one-hundred-hour war—using only volunteer troops)[13]

- an unprecedented multinational military coalition[14]

- unprecedented American military medical problems resulting from the war[15]

- unprecedented air warfare, using modern war technology[16]

- unprecedented precision weapons use[17]

- unprecedented live media war coverage[18]

- billed as "the most successful war fought by the United States in the 20th century."[19]

SEPTEMBER 11, 2001, TERRORIST ATTACKS

In this unparalleled event of mass mainland terrorism, aimed specifically at New York City and Washington, D.C., America suffered its greatest loss of human life ever in such an assault. The resulting shock waves reverberated around the world, but particularly in the

Middle East. To date, this event still stands as the deadliest international terrorist attack in world history.[20] It certainly qualifies as an unprecedented, horrifying world event.

EVER SINCE 9/11

More than a dozen years later, as of the writing of this book, America is still heavily engaged in the Middle East and Afghanistan. The current engagement was undeniably initiated by the events of that specific day in 2001. The combined loss of human life (American and enemy combatants) since that date, as a direct result of the ensuing war(s), has been in the tens of thousands, and continues to rise.[21]

There are many who believe that if there is to be a dreaded World War III, it will have had its roots in the first Gulf War and the subsequent terrorist attacks of September 11, 2001. If these events did set in motion a chain reaction of other events leading to a cataclysmic World War III—certainly, there would be an undeniable connection of biblical proportions.

What if each of these events were tied together through the prophetic proclamations of a single document known to humankind, written well over two thousand years ago? Furthermore, what if most of these unprecedented occurrences were linked by *key words* embedded in that ancient document—coded with apparent specificity—yet revealed to the world only in the last hundred years or so?

Read on—you may be stunned by what you discover in the incredible journey that follows.

8

BIBLICAL TRUMPETS

I was in the Spirit on the Lord's Day, and heard behind me a
great voice, as of a trumpet.

—REVELATION 1:10

As we begin our study of the use of trumpets in the Bible, it
is essential that we first take a quick look at the importance
of the number seven and, in particular, its biblical theme of
supernatural identification.

The number seven (or the word *seventh*, or multiples of
seven) is found several hundred times in the Bible, from
Genesis to Revelation. Some estimates mark the number's appearance at over eight hundred. The book of Revelation alone uses the
number seven more than fifty times! The first use of the word *seven*
(seventh) is found in the opening verses of Genesis 2: "Thus the

heavens and the earth were finished, and all the host of them. And on the *seventh day* God ended his work which he had made; and he rested on the seventh day from all his work which he had made. And God blessed the seventh day, and sanctified it: because that in it he had rested from all his work which God created and made" (vv. 1–3, emphasis added).

We discover in these verses that the number seven indicates perfection and completeness. When we examine the scores of scriptural uses of the number seven, it is clear that it is prevalently used in this manner. There is even a surprising occasion in which the number seven shows up in the Bible but is actually unseen in the English text—yet its presence is one of the most beautiful presentations of completeness and perfection in the entirety of Scripture.

The first verse of the Bible is made up of ten English words: "In the beginning God created the heavens and the earth." However, in the original language of the book of Genesis, this verse is composed of *seven* Hebrew words: *Bereisheet bara Elohim et hashamayim ve'et ha'aretz.* Amazingly, the message of the very first verse is that of completion, perfection, and God's divine touch—and it just happens to be given to us in exactly seven original Hebrew words! One cannot get past the first verse of the Bible without running into the profound significance of the number seven. As our study continues, you will discover further significance of this number as it relates to the Revelation trumpet visions.

TRUMPETS IN THE BIBLE

Since our focus is that of the seven trumpets of Revelation, let us first have a look at the general subject of trumpets as they are contextually used throughout God's Word. This will aid us in our interpretation of the trumpet visions found in Revelation.

The Bible's word *trumpet*, as it is used in the Old Testament, actually refers to an ancient musical instrument known as the *shofar*. The shofar used by the Jewish people is most often made from a ram's horn, though it can be made from the horn of a sheep or a goat as well. The shofar makes a deep, throaty, blasting, and trumpetlike sound. The person who blows the shofar is called a *Tokea,* which is Hebrew for "blaster."

Blowing the shofar is no easy assignment, especially when skillfully crafting each of the commonly recognized sounds the simple instrument can produce. The blast of the shofar resonating through the mountains and valleys of the ancient land of Israel would have been a fearsome and awe-inspiring sound.

According to the renowned Jewish philosopher Maimonides, the sound of the shofar on Rosh Hashanah (the Feast of Trumpets) was meant to wake up the soul and turn it toward repentance.[1]

THE PRECEDENT TRUMPET

The first time the word *trumpet* is used in the Bible is in the book of Exodus. In this passage we are taken to the foot of Mount Sinai into the fearful presence of the Lord as He instructs Moses concerning His impending appearance to the people of the Exodus.

> And be ready against the third day: for the third day the LORD will come down in the sight of all the people upon mount Sinai. And thou shalt set bounds unto the people round about, saying, Take heed to yourselves, that ye go not up into the mount, or touch the border of it: whosoever toucheth the mount shall be surely put to death: There shall not an hand touch it, but he shall surely be stoned, or shot through; whether it be beast or man, it shall not live: *when the trumpet soundeth* long, they shall come up to the mount. And Moses went down from the mount unto the people, and sanctified the people; and they washed their clothes.
> —EX. 19:11–14, *emphasis added*

The premier trumpet's use was not as a call to the lost, or pagans living in proximity to God's people. No, the trumpet sound was meant to exclusively direct the attention of God's "called-out ones" toward the particular thing the Lord would do in a focused arena. In

Exodus 19, He was going to pronounce *the law* to His people. They were to be the new nation, and He wanted their undivided attention.

Interestingly, the very last time the word *trumpet* is used in the New Testament before arriving at the book of Revelation is in the book of Hebrews. And this use of the word refers all the way back to the first use of the word in Exodus!

> For ye are not come unto the mount that might be touched, and that burned with fire, nor unto blackness, and darkness, and tempest, and the sound of a trumpet, and the voice of words; which voice they that heard entreated that the word should not be spoken to them any more.
>
> —HEB. 12:18–19

The last use of the word *trumpet* is found in Revelation 11, and it is used in direct connection with the seven trumpet visions of Revelation. What do we discover about the predominant purpose for which trumpets are generally used in the Bible? Following is a synopsis of the biblical use of the word *trumpet*:

An Announcement of a Celebration or Feast
Then shalt thou cause the trumpet of the jubilee to sound on the tenth day of the seventh month, in the Day of Atonement shall ye make the trumpet sound throughout all your land.

—LEV. 25:9

A Call to Gather
And if they blow but with one trumpet, then the princes, which are heads of the thousands of Israel, shall gather themselves unto thee.

—NUM. 10:4

A Call to Battle
When I blow with a trumpet, I and all that are with me, then
blow ye the trumpets also on every side of all the camp, and say,
The sword of the LORD, and of Gideon.

—JUDG. 7:18

A Declaration of Victory
And Jonathan smote the garrison of the Philistines that was in
Geba, and the Philistines heard of it. And Saul blew the trumpet
throughout all the land, saying, Let the Hebrews hear.

—1 SAM. 13:3

A Sound of Victory in Worship
So David and all the house of Israel brought up the ark of the
LORD with shouting, and with the sound of the trumpet.

—2 SAM. 6:15

Pronouncing a New King
And let Zadok the priest and Nathan the prophet anoint him
there king over Israel: and blow ye with the trumpet, and say,
God save king Solomon.

—1 KINGS 1:34

An Instrument of Warning for God's People
For the builders, every one had his sword girded by his side, and
so builded. And he that sounded the trumpet was by me.

—NEH. 4:18

A Sign That the Lord Is Always Victorious
God is gone up with a shout, the LORD with the sound of a
trumpet. Sing praises to God, sing praises: sing praises unto our
King, sing praises.

—PS. 47:5–6

An Alarm of War
I am pained at my very heart; my heart maketh a noise in me; I cannot hold my peace, because thou hast heard, O my soul, the sound of the trumpet, the alarm of war.

—JER. 4:19

A Call to Repentance
Also I set watchmen over you, saying, Hearken to the sound of the trumpet. But they said, We will not hearken.

—JER. 6:17

The Declaration of God's Coming Wrath
Son of man, speak to the children of thy people, and say unto them, When I bring the sword upon a land, if the people of the land take a man of their coasts, and set him for their watchman: If when he seeth the sword come upon the land, he blow the trumpet, and warn the people; Then whosoever heareth the sound of the trumpet, and taketh not warning; if the sword come, and take him away, his blood shall be upon his own head.

—EZE. 33:2–4

A Sound of Alarm for "the Day of the Lord"
Blow ye the trumpet in Zion, and sound an alarm in my holy mountain: let all the inhabitants of the land tremble: for the day of the LORD cometh, for it is nigh at hand.

—JOEL 2:1

The great day of the LORD is near, it is near, and hasteth greatly, even the voice of the day of the LORD: the mighty man shall cry there bitterly. That day is a day of wrath, a day of trouble and distress, a day of wasteness and desolation, a day of darkness and gloominess, a day of clouds and thick darkness, a day of the trumpet and alarm against the fenced cities, and against the high towers.

—ZEPH. 1:14–16

And then shall appear the sign of the Son of man in heaven: and then shall all the tribes of the earth mourn, and they shall see the Son of man coming in the clouds of heaven with power and great glory. And he shall send his angels with a great sound of a trumpet, and they shall gather together his elect from the four winds, from one end of heaven to the other.

—MATT. 24:30–31

* * *

The preponderance of the uses of the word *trumpet* in the Bible specifically calls for the attention of God's people. Certainly others who were in the vicinity of the people of God might "hear the trumpet" as well. However, in the vast majority of cases, the shofar was blown for the sole purpose of relaying a certain message, or a call to action, for the people of God.

Equipped with the entirety of the foregoing information, we should approach the seven trumpets of Revelation, at least from the start, with the same understanding we have gleaned from our contextual study of the scriptural use of trumpets. After all, it would be highly unlikely that God's Word would present such a definitive concept in practically the same way throughout the entirety of the Bible then suddenly change the context, and only in the book of Revelation, without a thorough explanation of the change.

Let us now examine a fascinating biblical possibility—that the general layout of the storyline of the book of Revelation corresponds to the feasts of the Lord, and particularly to the Feast of Trumpets.

9

THE FEASTS OF THE LORD AND THE BOOK OF REVELATION

And I heard a great voice out of heaven saying, Behold, the tabernacle of God is with men.

—REVELATION 21:3

n Leviticus 23, the Lord prescribed a unique feast to be commemorated on one very specific day. It was one of seven holy feasts given at Mount Sinai to the nation of Israel. That feast was called the Feast of Trumpets, or *Yom Teruah*. Here were God's instructions:

Speak unto the children of Israel, saying, In the *seventh month*, in *the first day* of the month, shall ye have a sabbath, a memorial of blowing of trumpets, an holy convocation.

—LEV. 23:24; *emphasis added*

Notice that the trumpets were to be blown on only *one* day of the year: the first day of the seventh month. There is that number seven again—this time affiliated with the Feast of Trumpets.

THE FEAST OF TRUMPETS

According to the scriptural command, this particular day of trumpet blowing was to serve as a warning sound and a call to preparation—leading up to the coming Feast of Atonement, or the Day of Atonement, known in Hebrew as Yom Kippur.

The Day of Atonement is also known among the Jews as the Day of Judgment. Simply put, this was the one and only day within each year that the high priest would enter the Holy of Holies to make atonement for the sins of the nation. If God accepted their sacrifice, they were under His "salvation" for another year. If He did not accept the sacrifice, they were under his "wrath."

It is because of this clear picture (of the warning of the final wrath to come) that many examiners of Revelation understand its seven trumpets to perfectly represent the final fulfillment of the Feast of Trumpets. Right after the seventh trumpet of Revelation, the angels are ordered to pour out even more judgment—seven vials, or bowls, of His wrath—on the unbelieving world (Rev. 16).

The Feast of Trumpets, as practiced among the Jews today, is filled with diverse traditions. Those traditions fluctuate slightly, depending on the particular sect to which one belongs or which rabbinical teaching one elevates over another, but the general celebration is held over a period of two days, instead of the biblically prescribed single day (though there is evidence that the Feast of Trumpets was celebrated in Israel on only a single day as late as the thirteenth century[1]).

In Leviticus 23, strangely, God says nothing about a specific number of trumpet blasts during the feast. There are now a series of at least one hundred trumpet blasts prescribed to be blown on each of the two days of the more modern rendition of its celebration. Specific notes and patterns with accompanying traditional symbolism stipulate each blast. The last trumpet blown on each day is often referred to as the *tekiah gedolah*. In English this would translate to the *big shofar blast*. There are certain commemorations, games, foods, and scripture readings that are approved for the celebration of this day as well.

Some rabbinical sects teach that the Day of Trumpets is set aside for the purpose of celebrating the exact day of the creation of the universe. Others teach that it is the specific celebration of the creation of mankind.

Most Jewish sects hold to strict teachings about the various levels of repentance and covering to which one can attain during Trumpets—just before the Day of Atonement. However, all of the aforementioned are mere traditions that have been *added* to the simple and clear biblical command. These customs have been added over many centuries, through the teachings of the rabbis in the Mishnah[2] and the Talmud.[3]

The Feast of Trumpets is known among the Jews of today as Rosh Hashanah. It is on this day that the official Jewish New Year is celebrated. Again, this is not a specific biblical command—but one of rabbinical tradition—and one that is held in high esteem by the Jewish people.

THE SEVEN FEASTS OF THE LORD

SPRING FEASTS	EARLY SUMMER FEAST	FALL FEASTS
PASSOVER JESUS CRUCIFIED		**TRUMPETS** TO BE FULFILLED
UNLEAVENED BREAD IN THE TOMB	**PENTECOST** CHURCH BORN	**DAY OF ATONEMENT** TO BE FULFILLED
FIRST FRUITS RESURRECTION		**TABERNACLES** TO BE FULFILLED

THE FIRST FOUR FEASTS

Most serious students of the Bible are aware that Jesus' ministry of reconciliation and the gospel message precisely fulfill the anciently prescribed feasts of the Lord. Passover, the first feast, was perfectly fulfilled in Jesus' sacrifice on the cross. It was there that the final and ultimate Lamb of God was given for the covering of all who would come under His blood of forgiveness (1 Cor. 5:7). As a matter of fact, the ancient biblical prescription of placing the blood of the Passover lamb upon the head of the door frame and the two doorposts formed the perfect shape of a bloodstained cross!

Additionally, the rabbinical tradition of celebrating the Passover Seder ends with a dessert composed of a bit of unleavened bread, called *afikoman*, which is secreted away in the pocket of a white linen cloth then hidden in some inconspicuous place in the house. The children search the house until they find the cloth with the hidden bread. In actuality, the word *afikoman* has little to do with dessert. The word, often written in Hebrew, actually derives from the Greek verb *afikomenos,* which means "the Coming One" or "He who has come." It can also be translated as "It is completed" or "It is finished."[4] In the modern celebration of Passover, even the Orthodox Jew unknowingly pronounces the heart of the gospel message of Jesus Christ!

Further, we know that Jesus fulfilled the Feast of Unleavened Bread (Matt. 26:26) in that He is the ultimate bread without yeast and the very bread of life itself—the bread of eternal sustenance. At His last Passover meal with the disciples, He declared concerning the bread, "Take, eat; this is my body."

We also know that Jesus fulfilled the Feast of Firstfruits in that this was the exact day upon which Jesus arose from the dead. It is for this reason that the apostle Paul declared Jesus to be the *firstborn from the dead* and the *firstfruits of them that slept* (Col. 1:15–18; 1 Cor. 15:20).

Additionally, we are aware that the church was born on the Feast of Pentecost as outlined in Acts 2. At the giving of the Holy Spirit and the ingathering of the new harvest through the preaching of the gospel on that day, the biblically prescribed feast was ultimately fulfilled.

THE REMAINING THREE FEASTS AND REVELATION

Since the first four feasts were so precisely fulfilled in Jesus Christ and the birth of the church, should not the remaining three feasts be satisfied with similar precision? The logical answer would appear to be yes.

Consequently, we have three feasts yet to be *ultimately* fulfilled: Trumpets, Atonement, and Tabernacles. And it should come as no surprise that the book of Revelation appears to follow a perfect time-line schematic for the fulfillment of these remaining three great feasts!

The Feast of Atonement, as previously stated, is the holiest day of the year for the Jewish people. It is upon this day that the High Priest of Israel would enter the Holy of Holies to make atonement for the sins of the people. If God accepted this sacrifice, then they were "under the blood" and were covered, or protected, for another full year from God's wrath and judgment.

The Feast of Tabernacles, or Sukkot, lasts seven days. It is the last of the seven feasts and commemorates the people of God, delivered from Egypt under the blood of the sacrificial lamb, now dwelling together with the Lord in His safety and under His provision.

Consider for a moment: by the time we were given the book of Revelation, the first four feasts were already fulfilled. The book of Revelation has now been given specifically for the church (the seven letters to the seven churches).

When the seals of the Revelation scroll are opened by the Lamb on the throne, giving the general clues of the unfolding future and the end-times—what is the general chronological teaching of Revelation from there? Is it not that, first, a series of trumpets will blow (the seven trumpets), followed by God's great day of judgment (the seven vials, or bowls, of wrath), to be ultimately followed by the millennial reign and the new heaven and the new earth in which

God dwells (tabernacles) with His redeemed people? Can you not see the pattern in Revelation of the Feast of Trumpets, followed by the Feast of Atonement (Day of Judgment), culminating in the Feast of Tabernacles (God dwelling with His people)? The pattern is obvious. The last hint of these "feast fulfillments" in Revelation is found in some of its closing words:

> And I heard a great voice out of heaven saying, Behold, *the tabernacle of God is with men*, and he will dwell with them, and they shall be his people, and God himself shall be with them, and be their God. And God shall wipe away all tears from their eyes; and there shall be no more death, neither sorrow, nor crying, neither shall there be any more pain: for the former things are passed away.
>
> —REV. 21:3–4; *emphasis added*

Since the book of Revelation is Jesus' final prophetic word to His church, then it makes sense that He might reveal what the remaining three feasts of the Lord would look like in their ultimate fulfillment. It is for this biblical and logical reason that many believe we might now be living in the Feast of Trumpet days—the seven (complete and perfect) trumpets of Revelation!

Let us now turn our attention to a particularly striking biblical fact regarding a seven trumpet series in the Old Testament. The following chapter lays out an important consideration often overlooked by Revelation interpreters. And this really is no small matter.

10

AND THE WALLS CAME TUMBLING DOWN

Shout; for the LORD hath given you the city.

—JOSHUA 6:16

The fact of the matter is that there is only one other place in the entirety of the Bible where a series of trumpet blasts from seven specific trumpets is set forth. This sounding of seven trumpets is found in the book of Joshua.

THE SEVEN-TRUMPET SERIES OF THE OLD TESTAMENT

It would be of monumental contextual significance to discover what the message of the Old Testament's "seven trumpets" was about before proceeding to decode the meaning of the New Testament's "seven trumpets." This is the proper and contextual way to begin a study of the Bible. Observe these selected Old Testament passages from the book of Joshua (emphasis added):

> And the LORD said unto Joshua, See, I have given into thine hand Jericho, and the king thereof, and the mighty men of valour. And ye shall compass the city, all ye men of war, and go round about the city once. Thus shalt thou do six days. And *seven priests* shall bear before the ark *seven trumpets of rams' horns*: and the seventh day ye shall compass the city seven times, and the priests shall blow with the trumpets. And it shall come to pass, that when they make a long blast with the ram's horn, and when ye hear the sound of the trumpet, all the people shall shout with a great shout; and the wall of the city shall fall down flat, and the people shall ascend up every man straight before him.
>
> —JOSHUA 6:2–5, *emphasis added*

> And *seven priests* bearing *seven trumpets* of rams' horns before the ark of the LORD went on continually, and blew with the trumpets: and the armed men went before them; but the reward came after the ark of the LORD, the priests going on, and blowing with the trumpets. And the second day they compassed the city once, and returned into the camp: so they did six days. And it came to pass on the *seventh day*, that they rose early about the dawning of the day, and compassed the city after the same manner seven times: only on that day they compassed the city seven times. *And it came to pass at the seventh time, when the priests blew with the trumpets, Joshua said unto the people, Shout; for the Lord hath given you the city.*
>
> —JOSHUA 6:13–16, *emphasis added*

Based on the foregoing scriptures, the Old Testament rendition of a seven trumpet series can be described thus: Jericho represented the obstacle confronting God's people that kept them from simply marching in and inheriting the Land of Promise. Jericho was a formidable city. The settlement was walled with thick battlements and staffed with mighty warriors to defend its people and property. Humanly speaking, it was impossible for any ordinary army to easily penetrate its fortresses and defeat the city. But God had a plan. The Lord of Hosts would bring down this seemingly impenetrable fortress with supernatural intervention, and God's people would then go "up" and inherit the Promised Land.

Furthermore, this supernatural day of the Lord—a victory for God's people—would be marked by the blowing of seven trumpets in the hands of seven priests, much like the seven trumpets of Revelation in the hands of the seven angels from God's throne.

The trumpet blasts would serve a twofold purpose. First, they would signify to God's people that the Lord would soon display His power and fulfill His promise. Every time the trumpets were blasted, His people took courage. God was reminding the Israelites that He was in control of the ostensibly impossible situation. He had made a promise to His people, and they could depend on Him to keep it. The trumpet blasts ominously sounded that promise.

Second, the sound of the trumpets was to serve as a warning to the citizens of the walled and evil city that the judgment of almighty God would soon fall on them.

More than likely, the people of Jericho imagined the mere blowing of trumpets to be utterly foolish. Even though the shofar blasts were harbingers of an ominous judgment soon to come, the trumpet sounds were largely ignored and even mocked by the obstinate people behind the immense walls of Jericho.

However, at the end of it all, the people under the soon-coming judgment could never say they had not been warned. They could never deny that they had seen the priests and heard the sound of the blaring shofar. Neither could the people of God deny, on the day the walls fell, that the barriers fell at the promise of God Himself—precisely at the sounding of the trumpet blasts, and in particular on the seventh and final day.

THE JERICHO TRUMPETS—THE REVELATION TRUMPETS

The seven trumpets of Jericho serve as a "type" of the seven trumpets of Revelation. Contextually speaking, they almost have to be interpreted in this manner, in that they are the only two models, in all of God's Word, of a series of seven trumpets. Accordingly, the second model must be examined by first understanding the premier model, found here, in the book of Joshua. When this is done, the biblical and contextual similarities between the two seven-trumpet models are astounding.

When making these comparisons, it could thus be interpreted that the first six trumpets of Revelation are sounds of the promise and the warning of the soon-coming destruction of this world system (the modern Jericho) in the very last days. The "Jericho world system" is the one thing that stands between God's people and the final prophetic fulfillment of God dwelling with His people in a re-created paradise (the ultimate Promised Land). The six trumpets were to sound on different "days" or in different epochs of time as the world system quickly draws to a close in the last days. Even though the trumpets are blown by angels (heavenly messengers) in Revelation, they are supposed to be announced to the world by God's people (the church)—symbolically marching around the soon-to-be doomed city of Jericho, that is, the godless, last-days world system.

Accordingly, the trumpet harbingers of Revelation would need to be unprecedented events—proceedings so large that no one could miss them once properly interpreted and understood. They would have to be of such a monumental nature that God's people could clearly see them, once they were properly directed to understand them, and even the unbelieving world would have a hard time explaining them away after being accurately revealed.

And then there is the seventh trumpet. Just as the seventh day of the trumpets of Jericho represented the victory for God's people and their ability to "go up" into the Promised Land, many believe the seventh trumpet of Revelation signifies the rapture of the church just before God pours out His wrath on those left behind. Even the apostle Paul spoke of this truth. He clearly revealed a biblical "mystery" associated with a "last trumpet." But . . . of which "last trumpet" was Paul speaking?

The next chapter will unravel that mystery.

11

PAUL'S MYSTERIOUS LAST TRUMPET

Behold, I shew you a mystery; we shall not all sleep, but we shall all be changed, in a moment, in the twinkling of an eye, at the last trump: for the trumpet shall sound, and the dead shall be raised incorruptible, and we shall be changed.

—1 CORINTHIANS 15:51–52

A great surprise to a number of Bible students is the discovery that Paul had a full revelation of the end-times—in vision form—*before* the apostle John's famous Patmos vision, which resulted in the book of Revelation. This fact is immensely important in that, once we are armed with this information, we can use Paul's words to shine interpretation assistance upon John's words—and vice versa.

This truth becomes extremely important when considering John's vision of the seven trumpets given in the book of Revelation—because Paul spoke several times about trumpets in his writings, particularly in the books of 2 Corinthians and 2 Thessalonians.

It is commonly accepted among leading Bible scholars that John's revelation on Patmos occurred around AD 95. The earliest that most reputable scholars would date the book of Revelation is around AD 70. The point is that the apostle Paul died in AD 67—anywhere from three to twenty-eight years before John would have his Revelation vision.

Now, here is where our study becomes fascinating. Twice in the New Testament, Paul mentioned a period of "fourteen years." The two references to these dates appear to be connected. This particular time frame thus becomes an important detail of consideration.

In the book of Galatians, we find Paul giving his personal testimony of faith. He revealed that after his Damascus Road conversion experience, it was *three years* before he went to the church at Jerusalem to become acquainted with Peter, the chief pastor, along with James and John. Paul then stated it was a full *fourteen years* after that (apparently some seventeen years after his conversion) before he went back to the church at Jerusalem, with Barnabas, to disclose his calling from God to preach the gospel among the Gentiles. This calling, he said, was given to him by a revelation from the Lord.

> But when God, who set me apart from birth and called me by his grace, was pleased to reveal his Son in me so that I might preach him among the Gentiles, I did not consult any man, nor did I go up to Jerusalem to see those who were apostles before I was, but I went immediately into Arabia and later returned to Damascus. *Then after three years, I went up to Jerusalem* to get acquainted with Peter and stayed with him fifteen days. I saw none of the other apostles—only James, the Lord's brother. I assure you before God that what I am writing you is no lie. Later I went to Syria and Cilicia. I was personally unknown to the churches of Judea that are in Christ. They only heard the report: "The man who formerly persecuted us is now preaching the faith he once tried to destroy." And they praised God because of me. *Fourteen years later* I went up again to Jerusalem, this time with Barnabas. I took Titus along also. *I went in response to a revelation* and set

before them the gospel that I preach among the Gentiles. But I did this privately to those who seemed to be leaders; for fear that I was running or had run my race in vain.

—GAL. 1:15–2:2 NIV; *emphasis added*

The apostle Paul's Damascus Road conversion experience is often estimated to have been between the years AD 33 and 36.[1] Remember, however, that these dates are only estimates. Even the best of scholars are not in absolute agreement on the dates.

Next, we will read Paul's words to the church at Corinth in his second letter to that church. Again, the date ranges for the writing of this letter vary among scholars. Some date it as soon as the early AD 50s, and others date it near the end of the 50s. Most date it in the middle 50s. But if you do the math, you can see that the vision Paul spoke of in 2 Corinthians falls easily into the same time frame as Paul's conversion experience and the subsequent vision of which he wrote in the book of Galatians.

It is fairly safe to say that these two mentions of a vision are probably the same event in Paul's life. But what exactly was this magnificent vision of which Paul spoke? Let us read his own words:

It is not expedient for me doubtless to glory. I will come to visions and revelations of the Lord. I knew a man in Christ above *fourteen years ago*, (whether in the body, I cannot tell; or whether out of the body, I cannot tell: God knoweth;) such a one caught up to the third heaven. And I knew such a man, (whether in the body, or out of the body, I cannot tell: God knoweth;) how that he was caught up into paradise, and heard unspeakable words, which it is not lawful for a man to utter.

—2 COR. 12:1–4; *emphasis added*

The exact date of Paul's vision is not absolutely necessary. Paul assures us that it *did* happen, and we know he died by AD 67. So the event took place sometime before then. The amazing fact Paul revealed to us is that he was caught up to Paradise! This is exactly what John described as happening to him three decades later. Paul hinted that he was more than likely "in the Spirit" when he was taken into the presence of the throne room of God, the third heaven.

While in that rapturous state, Paul informs us, he was privy to heavenly revelations that were unspeakable. That is, the words were beyond his imagination or perfect human explanation. He was thrust into the future—perhaps thousands of years into the future and into the last days. How can we be certain of this? Because Paul wrote prolifically about the rapture of the church, the trumpets of the last days, the return of the saints with the conquering Jesus, our glorified bodies, our eternal state of bliss, and many other end-time details.

Apparently, Paul was not given the responsibility to expose the specific prophetic timeline of end-time events—that task would fall, at a later time, to the apostle John. But what Paul *was* allowed to share, he did reveal—and because of it we are much richer in our understanding of eschatology.

Many are convinced these next words of Paul were penned precisely because of what he experienced while in his state of a heavenly vision, when he was *caught up* to the third heaven—in the Spirit:

> But as it is written, Eye hath not seen, nor ear heard, neither have entered into the heart of man, the things which God hath prepared for them that love him. But God hath revealed them unto us by his Spirit: for the Spirit searcheth all things, yea, the deep things of God.
>
> —1 COR. 2:9–10

It appears Paul was trying to tell his audience something like this: "It is impossible to describe the future events of the world or the future state of the believer who is in Christ. I have seen it all. I was caught up to Paradise. The earthbound, human mind cannot conceive of what lies ahead! However, the Spirit of God can make known to us things we need to know. He has done this with me, and now I am sharing with you what I have seen and what I was allowed to give to you."

PAUL SPOKE OF A "LAST TRUMPET"

Paul connected the sounding of a trumpet (shofar) with the rapture of the saints, or the rapture of the church. Specifically, in one of his verses, he identified that certain trumpet which signals the rapture as the last trumpet.

Here is an interesting numerical identification that Paul reveals. The word *last* indicates there has to be a series of at least two trumpets. There would have to be, at the very least, a first and an ending trumpet for Paul to specify that something definitive will happen at the "last" trumpet blast. The problem is that Paul did not give us a list, or a series, of trumpets in any of his writings. However, we can be assured he knew about a certain series of trumpets, and that the last one in that series will be the signal of the saints of God being caught up to be with the Lord.

This last trumpet of which Paul spoke will be the last one in a specific holy series of trumpets. I am convinced that, years later, the Lord brought the apostle John up to that same Paradise, the third heaven, and revealed to him the same series of trumpets that was revealed to Paul much earlier. With John, however, the Lord revealed the whole series, the seven trumpets of Revelation, and gave him the assignment of listing them and greatly elucidating them.

If these biblical assumptions are correct, then the last trumpet of which Paul spoke would correlate with the seventh trumpet of Revelation. This is the only series of trumpet blasts with which we are familiar in the New Testament times. And the last trumpet of that series is the seventh trumpet. Observe the words of Paul associating this particular trumpet with the rapture of the church and the return of the Lord Jesus Christ:

> Behold, I shew you a mystery; we shall not all sleep, but we shall all be changed, in a moment, in the twinkling of an eye, *at the last trump*: for the trumpet shall sound, and the dead shall be raised incorruptible, and we shall be changed. For this corruptible must put on incorruption, and this mortal must put on immortality.
>
> —1 COR. 15:51–53; *emphasis added*

In the book of Thessalonians, written earlier than the second letter to the church at Corinth, Paul again mentioned the sounding of a trumpet in connection to the rapture of God's people:

> For the Lord himself shall descend from heaven with a shout, with the voice of the archangel, and *with the trump of God*: and the dead in Christ shall rise first: Then we which are alive and remain shall be caught up together with them in the clouds, to meet the Lord in the air: and so shall we ever be with the Lord. Wherefore comfort one another with these words.
>
> —1 THESS. 4:16–18; *emphasis added*

The bottom line is this: John said there is a series of seven holy trumpet blasts. He listed them for us in the book of Revelation. The writing of John is the inspired Word of God. Paul, who also gave us the inspired Word of God, tells us the *last* of the trumpets (of a certain unnamed series) is the signal for the rapture of the saints.

THE GREAT TRUMP?

Not everyone agrees that the trumpet Paul mentioned will usher in the rapture. One prominent and decidedly pre-tribulation author categorically dismisses, with the following words, all the contextual possibilities that have just been laid out concerning the last trumpet that Paul presents: "Those in confusion interpret that the Rapture will happen after the seventh trumpet [of Revelation] sounds, since it's the last trumpet in a series of trumpets. This interpretation is in error." . . . The *great trump* [Paul's last trumpet] is blown at the second coming of Jesus Christ.[2]

All the author says is that Paul's last trumpet is the great trump, and if you do not believe this, then you are "confused" and "in error." That is not very helpful.

More than likely the author references what most who hold to the pre-tribulation rapture postulation identify as the "great trump" or the "great trumpet blast" or the very last trumpet of the Feast of Trumpets (the *tekiah gedolah*). We discussed this particular trumpet and the rabbinical (not necessarily biblical) traditions surrounding that feast in a previous chapter. You will also recall we discovered that the Feast of Trumpets appears to be specifically tied to the book of Revelation and the seven trumpet visions found in that book.

Those of the pre-tribulation persuasion make a complete disconnect between the Feast of Trumpets and the book of Revelation's vision of the seven trumpets. They proclaim that the last trumpet to which Paul actually referred is the last trumpet blown on the days of the rabbinically practiced Feast of Trumpets. However, many others see the distinct possibility that the Feast of Trumpets is symbolized in the seven trumpets of Revelation. Therefore the last of the seven revelation trumpets would specifically, and biblically, represent the *great trump*.

WHEN WE ASK THE BIBLE TO SPEAK...

When one simply allows the Bible to interpret the Bible—first and foremost—the picture is quite different from what the quoted author represents. Paul clearly and succinctly said the rapture will occur "at the last trumpet." When he used the word "last" he was speaking of a series of trumpets. The *only* series of trumpets laid out in the New Testament is the one found in Revelation—the seven trumpet visions. If it is indeed the last trumpet of the final series blown at the Feast of Trumpets, then that, too, wonderfully corresponds to the seven trumpets of Revelation.

Another stunning detail to consider is that John's last trumpet, the seventh trumpet of Revelation, is mentioned for the last time in Revelation 11. The Revelation 11 reference is, indeed, the very last time a trumpet is mentioned in the entirety of the Bible. It literally is *the last trumpet!* This actually *is* the great and *final trump* of the Bible.

Armed with this information, let us venture further into the potential meanings of the first six trumpets of Revelation. These trumpets could then be interpreted as certain events of the end-times, which could serve as holy announcements from the throne of

God, occurring sometime *before* the rapture of the church. Undoubtedly, the purpose of these announcements would be to proclaim the return of the Lord Jesus Christ is near! God's wrath is on its way!

12

UNDERSTANDING BIBLICAL REVELATION

Most people are bothered by those passages of Scripture they do not understand, but the passages that bother me are those I do understand.
—MARK TWAIN

T he concept of "biblical prophetic rhythm" is often a difficult one for some students of God's Word, but it is imperative that the serious Bible student understands it thoroughly. One cannot fully comprehend the book of Revelation, or any other truly prophetic passage, without being privy to this important key of interpretation.

THE REVELATORY STYLE OF HEBREW LITERATURE
The reader and expositor of Revelation is experiencing a common and well-documented revelatory style of Hebrew biblical literature.[1] The

unique Hebrew-Semitic style involves presentation ebb and flow, or a recapitulation, of the material presented. One of the easiest places to see this particular style is in the opening pages of Genesis.

AN EXAMPLE FROM GENESIS

In the Genesis creation account, the *entire* creation is first overviewed in Genesis 1:1. Next, the creation process is fully outlined in Genesis 1:2–2:2. Finally, in yet a third outline, the creation account is reiterated in Genesis 2:2–25. However, in this last account, a different but compatible viewpoint is brought forward, which runs concurrently with the previous two, yet with a slightly different and more detailed focus. This recapitulation process begins in Genesis, but it reappears throughout the Scripture in various places, especially the prophetic passages.

AN EXAMPLE FROM DANIEL

Another splendid Old Testament example of this style of *going forward and then backing up for a more focused view* is found in the book of Daniel. The chronological timeline of Daniel, chapter by chapter, is much too complex to reproduce here for ease of reading. However, a quick example, and one that is easy enough to plainly observe in the text, is that by the time we arrive at chapter 5, we find Belshazzar giving a decadent and prideful feast at which the "handwriting on the wall" appears.

We know from historical sources, and from the text of Daniel, that this event marked the fall of the Babylonian Empire to the Medo-Persian Empire. Daniel 6 opens with the account of the lion's den under King Darius the Mede. Yet, as chapter 7 opens we are sent all the way back to the first year of the reign of Belshazzar. This time period would be long before even the events of chapter 5. This ebb and flow of the account of Daniel is apparent several times within the book. Many Bible scholars believe the book of Revelation follows a similar oscillation process.

Once we recognize that this kind of revelatory presentation is common in biblical prophetic literature, we are better equipped to approach the book of Revelation. It is exactly this kind of ebb and flow of which the book of Revelation is made.

AN EXAMPLE FROM REVELATION

As a clear example of this oscillation process, consider the following Revelation scenario. In Revelation 6 we are introduced to the sixth of the seven seals from the scroll opened by the Lamb upon the throne. As the sixth seal is opened, it is announced that the "wrath of the Lamb" has come (v. 16). Accordingly, that would necessarily mean that seals one through five are cryptic representations of those things that will happen on the earth just before the wrath of the Lamb is poured out.

It also follows that the rapture of the church would happen sometime before this wrath is poured out, since we are promised in the Scriptures that the church will not undergo the final wrath of God (1 Thess. 5:9).

The fact must also be noted that those who hold to a pre-tribulation rapture argue that there is a difference between the wrath of the Lamb and the wrath of God. They make this distinction for an important reason, which I will point out momentarily.

However, numerous Bible scholars believe this emphatic distinction to be a grave and foundationally theological error because the Lamb *is* God! The Lamb is "God with us" (Matt. 1:22–23). Jesus said, "I and my Father are one" (John 10:30). To draw a difference between the wrath of the Lamb and the wrath of God, many believe, is a dangerous path on which to tread—and perhaps a mere distinction of necessity.

Furthermore, when one examines the text of the sixth seal in its entirety, there appears to be little doubt that the wrath referred to in this passage is none other than the great and final wrath of God that is to come upon the earth sometime after the church is raptured. As a matter of fact, just after this mention of the wrath of the Lamb, the passage further defines what that wrath is: "For the great day of *their* wrath has come" (v. 17 NIV; emphasis added). The same sentence that mentions the wrath of the Lamb also declares that the wrath is of the "face of him who sits on the throne" (NIV) as well. It appears to many Bible students as though the passage clearly defines itself, so there could be no mistaking that the wrath of the Lamb is the very same as the wrath of God. Read the passage for yourself:

> I watched as he opened the sixth seal. There was a great earth-quake. The sun turned black like sackcloth made of goat hair, the whole moon turned blood red, and the stars in the sky fell to earth, as late figs drop from a fig tree when shaken by a strong wind. The sky receded like a scroll, rolling up, and every moun-tain and island was removed from its place. Then the kings of the earth, the princes, the generals, the rich, the mighty, and every slave and every free man hid in caves and among the rocks of the mountains. They called to the mountains and the rocks, "Fall on us and hide us *from the face of him who sits on the throne and from the wrath of the Lamb! For the great day of their wrath has come,* and who can stand?"
>
> —REV. 6:12–17 NIV; *emphasis added*

Now comes the oscillation process that gives some students of Revelation a struggle. And this is precisely why certain eschatological schemes attempt to make the distinction between the wrath of the Lamb and the wrath of God.

Five chapters away, when we come to Revelation 11, we read again of the wrath of God being poured out upon an unrepentant mankind. This time, God's wrath is poured out right after the sev-enth trumpet. Many believe that trumpet signifies the rapture of the church:

> The seventh angel sounded his trumpet, and there were loud voices in heaven, which said: "The kingdom of the world has become the kingdom of our Lord and of his Christ, and he will

reign for ever and ever." And the twenty-four elders, who were seated on their thrones before God, fell on their faces and worshiped God, saying: "We give thanks to you, Lord God Almighty, the One who is and who was, because you have taken your great power and have begun to reign. The nations were angry; and your wrath has come. The time has come for judging the dead, and for rewarding your servants the prophets and your saints and those who reverence your name, both small and great—and for destroying those who destroy the earth."

—REV. 11:15–18 NIV

How can it be that there are two pronouncements that the wrath of God "has come"? The answer is not that there are two wraths. This is merely another example of the prophetic literature recapitulation or oscillation process previously noted. If you read Revelation in a strict chronological fashion, you will miss this feature, and that will cause interpretation problems.

Astute Revelation students immediately notice that as the sixth seal is opened, the rapture would have occurred and the Lamb's (God's) wrath has been poured out upon the earth. But they would also assert that with the opening of the seventh seal, we now have a *backing-up process* and a much closer focus upon those last days that lead up to the great and terrible day of God's wrath—the trumpet days.

PROGRESSIVE REVELATION—THE LAMB OF GOD

There is yet another important point to make regarding the proper interpretation of prophetic Scripture. What faithful student of God's Word does not remember Abraham's trek into the region of Moriah, where he was instructed to offer up his son Isaac as a sacrifice? It was at that spot, and upon Abraham's faithful following of God's instruction, that Isaac was "delivered back" to his father, and a sacrificial substitute for Isaac was offered by the hand of God Himself. A ram was revealed to Abraham, then laid upon the altar in Isaac's stead, after which Abraham declared that famous prophetic truth: "And Abraham called the name of that place Jehovah-jireh [The LORD

Will Provide]: as it is said to this day, In the mount of the LORD it shall be seen" (Gen. 22:14).

More than five hundred years later, when Moses delivered the children of Israel out of Egypt and into the land of salvation by the blood of a sacrificial lamb sprinkled over the doorpost of every believer's home, could not that holy act have been interpreted as the absolute fulfillment of Abraham's declaration? Certainly, it *could* have. After all, God had "provided a lamb" for the salvation of his people.

Additionally, Moses had talked with God in a burning bush at the foot of Mount Sinai toward Horeb at Sinai. Horeb, or Sinai, was actually called by Moses "the mountain of God" (Ex. 3:1). Could this be the mountain-of-the-Lord experience where God would provide the lamb of deliverance for His people by revealing to Moses what he must now do? Surely, there were those who declared this to be the fulfillment of Abraham's prophecy—especially after the Passover Lamb and Exodus event.

However, the prophecy would undergo yet another vein of fulfillment. Months later, in the wilderness, again at Mount Sinai, the mountain of God, Moses would be given the instructions for the tabernacle sacrificial system. The sacrificial system would include, of all things, the continual sacrificing of lambs upon the altar. These lamb sacrifices were to be conducted for the sins of the people and the sins of the nation. There it was! *There* was God's complete fulfillment of Abraham's prophecy of the Lamb of God's sacrifice! After all, the commandment for the lamb sacrifice had been given at the mountain of the Lord—Sinai. Right?

But wait! There would be still another fulfillment to unfold. King Solomon, David's son, would eventually build a temple of sacrifice. Solomon's temple was constructed, of all places, on Mount Moriah—the exact place of Abraham's offering of sacrifice and the place where Abraham declared, "On the mountain of the LORD it will be provided" (Gen. 22:14 NIV). Surely, this was the fulfillment! Certainly, there could be nothing greater in fulfillment of Abraham's words than for the temple of sacrifice to have been built precisely where Isaac was offered up. Correct? Wrong! It was only a partial fulfillment. The revelation was still unfolding to completion.

God was revealing Abraham's prophecy—progressively. He was still preparing His people, and the world, for the *real* thing—yet to come. Abraham's declaration was marching forward into fulfillment, but the actual fulfillment would not come for a little more than one thousand years later. The completion of Abraham's prophecy, and God's promise, would be fulfilled in the person of Jesus Christ upon Calvary's cross—the final and complete Lamb of God.

A full fifteen hundred years would pass from the time Abraham first uttered the prophecy until it was ultimately fulfilled in Jesus Christ. In the meantime, the prophecy went through several veins of fulfillment before it was finally and ultimately completed.

And where did the complete fulfillment actually take place? The final and real *Lamb of God* was sacrificed on Calvary's hill, in the same region—and some would speculate in the same spot—upon which Abraham had offered up his son, Isaac, to God. Abraham's prophecy had finally found its definitive completion.

We are on the other side of the ultimate fulfillment of the prophecy, so it is easy for us to see it and analyze it. However, if we put ourselves in the place of God's ancient people, it is doubtful that we would have been able to come close to imagining the definitive completion of the prophecy in the One who would come, born of a virgin, and be given up for us on an old, rugged cross. The Pharisees, the prophecy scholars of the New Testament days, certainly missed the whole interpretation of the matter.

Therefore, the matter of prophecy interpretation must be approached judiciously. The Bible, and particularly the book of Revelation, is not a crystal ball or a Ouija board. Prophecies are given, especially end-time prophecies, so that when they have reached their fulfillment, God's people will know that He is on His throne—and when He declares a thing, the thing *will* be accomplished, to perfection, and in God's perfect timing and manner!

THE JUDEO-ISRAEL-CENTRIC KEY TO INTERPRETATION

Another indispensable key to interpreting the book of Revelation is recognizing that it was written by a Jew (John) to the first-century church. The first-century church was almost exclusively Jewish for the first several decades of its existence. Even after the Gentiles were finally evangelized and brought into the church, largely through the efforts of the apostle Paul, the church thrived on the Jewish Scriptures (Old Testament), the Jewish prophecies (Old Testament), and the teachings of the apostles (all of them Jews). It was for this reason that many of Paul's writings to the churches of his day were taken up with the issues of Jewish tradition and how the Gentiles (and the pure gospel message) fit into that tradition.

Even what we call the New Testament documents (the new and additional scripture of the early church) were all written by Hebrews. Therefore, the book of Revelation, undeniably, has many Jewish elements attached to it. For example, there are numerous allusions in the book of Revelation to Daniel, Isaiah, and Zechariah.

The identification of God's two witnesses (see Revelation 11) as the olive tree and the lampstand come straight from the book of Zechariah. Additional understanding also comes from an earlier chapter in Revelation as well as a chapter in Romans. Our understanding of the Gentile occupation of the Temple Mount, spoken of in Revelation 11, also comes from the book of Daniel.

Furthermore, when John is shown the beast, or the Antichrist, in chapter 13, he is told the number of his name is 666. Many Bible students recognize the phrase "the number of his name" as more than likely referring to the ancient Jewish understanding of *Gematria*. Gematria is the early rabbinical Jewish practice of assigning specific numerical values to each of the Hebrew letters of the alphabet. With these numerical values, the rabbis who were trained in Gematria looked for hidden significance in the number of one's name, or in the numerical and mystical significance of a particular Hebrew word.

It is significant to remember when attempting to interpret prophecy that most of it centers on the Middle East, Israel, and Jerusalem. This is often a difficult thing to remember for many Westerners, particularly Americans, who continually look for biblical clues to their own role in end-time prophecy. While there may be indicators of such United States connections, it is my opinion that interpreting prophecy correctly must first involve examining the Middle East connection and, especially, the Israel connection.

THE SEALS, THE TRUMPETS, THE BOWLS

The whole of Revelation, especially after chapter 5, is to be interpreted specifically around the dominant visions, which comprise three groups of seven. They are the seven seals, the seven trumpets, and the seven bowls (or vials) of wrath.

Another key to interpreting the specific prophecies of the trumpet visions of Revelation is to understand that the trumpet visions are an actual component of the seal visions. The seventh seal is not an event in and of itself, but rather, it opens into the first trumpet and continues until the last trumpet is blown. In other words, all seven trumpets of Revelation are contained within the revelation of the seventh seal.

> And *when he had opened the seventh seal,* there was silence in heaven about the space of half an hour. And I saw the seven angels which stood before God; and to them were given *seven trumpets* . . . And the seven angels which had the seven trumpets prepared themselves to sound.
>
> —REV. 8:1–2, 6; *emphasis added*

The seven trumpets are presented in their entirety between chapters 8 and 11 of Revelation. However, between the sixth trumpet and the seventh trumpet there is much revelatory material. The sixth trumpet is last mentioned in chapter 9, verse 13, and the seventh trumpet does not sound until chapter 11, verse 15.

At the very least, it has occurred to many Bible scholars that the seal visions of Revelation present a general overview (yet filled with important clues) of those sweeping last-days events marking the time of the beginning of the birth pangs through the appearance of the Antichrist to the rapture of the church.

The seventh seal is a part of the ebb and flow of the prophetic vision. The seventh seal, which consists of the totality of the seven trumpets, represents a backing up, with a laser focus on those final years, involving the Antichrist and the rapture of the church. The blowing of the seven trumpets represents the very last generation before the wrath of God is poured out, and the holy warnings from heaven to that generation. And this concept lines up perfectly with the seven trumpets of Jericho, as well as the Feast of Trumpets.

In the same way the Genesis recapitulation layout has been previously demonstrated, many believe the three visions of seven (seals, trumpets, bowls) are to be interpreted similarly. The first six seals are a general warning of the end-times, largely mirrored in Jesus' end-time revelation declarations of Matthew 24. The seventh seal then opens and reveals all seven trumpets. Immediately after the seventh trumpet of Revelation 11:15 (actually *concurrent* with the seventh trumpet), the bowls of wrath are on their way to being poured out on the unbelievers who are left behind.

> And the nations were angry, *and thy wrath is come*, and the time of the dead, that they should be judged, and that thou shouldest give reward unto thy servants the prophets, and to the saints, and them that fear thy name, small and great; and shouldest destroy them which destroy the earth.
> —REV. 11:18; *emphasis added*

The seventh trumpet is particularly interesting. Reading its description, one would certainly think we might be looking at a mirror image of Paul's description of the rapture. Compare Paul's declaration of the rapture event in 1 Thessalonians with the seventh trumpet event described in Revelation 11:12–15:

For the Lord himself will come down from heaven, with a loud command, with the voice of the archangel and with the trumpet call of God, and the dead in Christ will rise first. After that, we who are still alive and are left will be caught up together with them in the clouds to meet the Lord in the air. And so we will be with the Lord forever.

—1 THESS. 4:16–17 niv

Then they heard a loud voice from heaven saying to them, "Come up here." And they [the two witnesses] went up to heaven in a cloud, while their enemies looked on. At that very hour there was a severe earthquake and a tenth of the city collapsed. Seven thousand people were killed in the earthquake, and the survivors were terrified and gave glory to the God of heaven. The second woe has passed; the third woe is coming soon. The seventh angel sounded his trumpet, and there were loud voices in heaven, which said: "The kingdom of the world has become the kingdom of our Lord and of his Christ, and he will reign for ever and ever."

—REV.11:12–15 niv

But to whom was the command "Come up here" directed in the book of Revelation? It was directed to the two witnesses. Who, or what, are they? Actually, the answer is specifically revealed within the pages of Scripture.

13

THE OLIVE TREE AND THE LAMPSTAND

Not every puzzle is intended to be solved. Some are in place to test your limits. Others are, in fact, not puzzles at all.

—VERA NAZARIAN, *The Perpetual Calendar of Inspiration*

Whenever we come upon a word that jumps off the page, causing us to say, "I wonder why something that specific is being said here," we must consider it a key to unlocking a mystery. Those clues can often find their interpretation directly from the Word of God itself. Let me give you a few illustrations.

And I will give power to my two witnesses, and they will prophesy for 1,260 days, clothed in sackcloth. These are the two olive trees and the two lampstands that stand before the Lord of the earth.

—REV. 11:3–4 NIV

This is a rather emphatic identification of the witnesses; would you not agree?

There is a companion Old Testament understanding to the vision of these two witnesses. Amazingly, they are also presented as the olive tree and the lampstand. The lampstand consists of two gold pipes.

> Then I asked the angel, "What are these *two olive trees* on the right and the left of *the lampstand*? Again I asked him, "What are these two olive branches beside the *two gold pipes* that pour out golden oil?" He replied, "Do you not know what these are?" "No, my lord," I said. So he said, "These are the two who are anointed to serve the Lord of all the earth."
>
> —ZECH. 4:11–14 NIV; *emphasis added*

In Revelation 11, we have a definitive statement about the two witnesses. We are told they are to be interpreted as the olive tree and the lampstand. Those are the definitions the Bible gives to the two witnesses. This is our key.

Even though some interpreters of Revelation declare these two witnesses to be two literal men (the original Greek text does not actually use the word *men*), we first, at least, must begin with what the Bible plainly says about the olive tree and the lampstand—would you not agree? Let the Bible speak about itself first—then we can explore our own interpretations. This is an important rule of proper biblical exploration.

So, what does the Bible first, and clearly, say about the olive tree and the lampstand?

THE OLIVE TREE

> After all, if you were cut out of an olive tree that is wild by nature, and contrary to nature were grafted into a cultivated olive tree, how much more readily will these, the natural branches, be grafted into their own olive tree! I do not want you to be ignorant of this mystery, brothers, so that you may not be conceited: *Israel* has experienced a hardening in part until the full number of the Gentiles has come in.
>
> —ROM. 11:24–25 NIV; *emphasis added*

The undeniable context in the Romans 11 passage is Paul's instruction concerning the Gentile believers who are now, in Christ, becoming a part of "Israel" (in the spiritual sense). Paul declared that it was part of God's plan from the beginning, a mystery now revealed, that the Jew and Gentile are becoming one in the family of God through Jesus Christ.

The witness of God came first to the Jews, through the Hebrews (Israel), and now comes to the Gentile world, which has been grafted in through the grace of God in Jesus Christ. The olive tree, at least, represents spiritual Israel—or those among the Hebrews who have been born again in Jesus Christ. Of this fact, there can be little doubt.

THE LAMPSTAND

> The mystery of the seven stars that you saw in my right hand and of the seven golden lampstands is this: The seven stars are the angels of the seven churches, and the seven *lampstands* are the seven *churches.*
>
> —REV. 1:20 NIV; *emphasis added*

Amazingly, the lampstand of Revelation 11 is defined within the book of Revelation itself! And it is the first and only place where the word is used in the New Testament in this regard. There could be no clearer definition given. The lampstand is the *church.* To define the word even more closely, the lampstand is identified not only as the church as a whole, but also as the very witness of the church! And again, this definition comes directly from the Word of God—in the book of Revelation.

> "To the angel of the church in Ephesus write: These are the words of him who holds the seven stars in his right hand and walks among *the seven golden lampstands*: I know your deeds, your hard work and your perseverance. I know that you cannot tolerate wicked men, that you have tested those who claim to be apostles but are not, and have found them false. You have persevered and have endured hardships for my name, and have not grown weary. Yet I hold this against you: You have forsaken your first love.

Remember the height from which you have fallen! Repent and do the things you did at first. If you do not repent, *I will come to you and remove your lampstand* from its place."

—REV. 2:1–5 NIV; *emphasis added*

BIBLICAL PERSONIFICATION

Since the Bible is so poignantly clear in its definition of the key words found in Revelation 11, many students of prophecy have made the determination that the two witnesses spoken of in the book of Revelation are none other than the restored nation of Israel in the last days (this would certainly be a marvelous witness to the world) and the triumphant New Testament, spirit-filled church proclaiming the gospel throughout the world.

Since much prophecy finds its fulfillment in multiple strains of reality—it could well be that there are also two literal men who will become witnesses to the world in the last days as well. However, the interpretation certainly does not have to include them.

The Bible is filled with symbolic presentation of subjects of which it speaks. After all, wisdom is personified as a woman in Proverbs, the church is often personified as the bride of Christ, trees are said to clap their hands, Jerusalem is personified as Ariel, sin is presented as a crouching lion, Satan is presented as a serpent or a dragon, and Paul identifies the Jews and Gentiles as having become "one man." Why could not Israel and the church be personified as two men standing as God's witnesses in the last days, without having to necessarily be two literal men? Of course they *could* be presented in such a manner and still do no violence to the biblical pattern of revelation.

However, if we start with the plain and clear Word of God, we get, at least, the beginning of our answer—the witnesses of God are Israel and the church. And this is not a far stretch at all, for this is what the two entities have *always* been!

Throughout the old covenant days, God specifically declared the nation of Israel was to be His witness unto all the earth, and especially a light to the Gentiles (Isaiah 43:10). The same was true of the new covenant days and the specified role of the church. Some of the last recorded words of Jesus to the fathers of the earliest church (His disciples) were: "It is not for you to know the times or dates the Father has set by his own authority. But you will receive power when the Holy Spirit comes on you; *and you [the church] will be my witnesses* in Jerusalem, and in all Judea and Samaria, and to the ends of the earth" (Acts 1:7–8 NIV; emphasis added).

Out of Israel, the church was born. Out of one witness of God, the other was brought forth—so that the two became one.

To further illuminate this truth of interpretation, consider the fact that there is only one other place in the Bible that mentions the olive tree and a lampstand as witnesses of the Lord's glory: the prophetic Old Testament book of Zechariah:

> Then the angel who talked with me returned and wakened me, as a man is wakened from his sleep. He asked me, "What do you see?" I answered, "I see a solid gold lampstand with a bowl at the top and seven lights on it, with seven channels to the lights. Also there are two olive trees by it, one on the right of the bowl and the other on its left." I asked the angel who talked with me, "What are these, my lord?" He answered, "Do you not know what these are?" "No, my lord," I replied. So he said to me, "This is the word of the LORD to Zerubbabel: 'Not by might nor by power, but by my Spirit,' says the LORD Almighty." . . . Again I asked him, "What are these *two olive branches* beside the *two gold pipes* that pour out golden oil?" He replied, "Do you not know what these are?" "No, my lord," I said. So he said, "These are the *two who are anointed to serve the Lord* of all the earth."
>
> —ZECH. 4:1–6, 12–14 NIV; *emphasis added*

What does this vision mean? More than likely it is a prophetic image of the coming of the Christ in the person of Jesus (the continual flow of oil and the eternal Light that was to come). But from where would the Messiah "come?" Obviously, the light would emanate from the two olive trees. But what are they? The two olive trees represent the nation of Israel (the seed of Abraham's promise) and the Word of God (the prophecies of the coming Christ—given through the Old Testament). Undeniably, from these two the Messiah would *come forth*.

Observe these next words of commentary regarding this passage. This commentary comes from a decidedly conservative Bible study ministry:

> Zechariah the prophet was commissioned during this restoration period to encourage the returned exiles to complete the rebuilding of the temple, which had run into difficulties because of Israel's lack of faithfulness (Hag. 1:1–6) and opposition from neighboring peoples (Neh. 4:1–14). . . . Ultimately, this points to the true Light who came into the world to shine forth God's grace and build a living temple to honor our Father (John 1:1–18; 1 Peter 2:1–5). By His Spirit, this Light would restore glory to His covenant people.[1]

Following is a commentary from *Barnes' Notes* on Zechariah 4. Observe how this renowned and conservative Bible scholar interprets the book of Revelation in light of the vision found in Zechariah:

> The candlestick is authoritatively interpreted for us, by the adoption of the symbol in the Revelation, where our Lord is exhibited "as walking in the midst of the seven golden candlesticks" <Rev. 1:13; 2:1>, and, it is said, "the seven candlesticks are the seven Churches" <Rev. 1:20>; and our Lord says to the Apostles, on whom He founded the Church; "Ye are the light of the world: men light a candle, and put it on a candlestick, and it giveth light to them that are in the house" (<Matt. 5:14-15>, compare <Phil 2:15>). Cyril: "The golden candlestick is the Church, as being honored in the world, most bright in virtues, raised on high exceedingly by the doctrines of the true knowledge of God."[2]

ARE THERE "FOUR" WITNESSES?

Note that in Zechariah as well as in Revelation, there is specific mention of two olive trees and two lampstands (or, in the case of Zechariah, two golden pipes feeding the lampstand). Some have been confused by the imagery, which presents two of each—seemingly indicating a total of four witnesses. In both Revelation and Zechariah, the four elements of two olive trees and two lampstands (or golden pipes) are finally stated to be only two entities. In Zechariah they are called the two "who are anointed to serve the Lord" (Zech. 4:14 NIV). In Revelation they are called the two witnesses that stand "before the God of the earth" (Rev. 11:4). In other words, the Zechariah vision appears to be the same as the Revelation vision.

The mystery is best explained something like this: The first singular witness, the olive tree, is made up of the nation of Israel as well as the Law and the Prophets (the Old Testament and the prophecies of the coming Christ). On the other hand, the second singular witness, the lampstand, is the church, built upon the foundation of the apostles (who came from Israel) and the redeemed "saints" (Jew and Gentile), filled with the Holy Spirit, which make up the body of Christ, of which Jesus is the Head. The Scripture declares that we, the New Testament born-again believers, are the new "temple" of God (1 Cor. 3:16–17; 6:19, 2 Cor. 6:16, Eph. 2:19–22).

It is also interesting to note that in Romans 11, Paul stated that the olive tree is Israel—yet that particular olive tree is made up of both Jew and the *ingrafted* Gentile, who become both the church and the "new" Israel—together. "In this way," declared Paul, "all *Israel* [in the spiritual sense] will be saved" (v. 26 NIV; emphasis added).

There well may appear two specific, and literal, men witnessing at the Western Wall or at a restored temple in Jerusalem in the last days—as one particular rapture proposal suggests. Then again, nowhere does the Scripture *demand* that a new temple be built, nor does it name the two supposed men witnesses, nor does it mention the Western Wall.

However, if we simply let the Scripture interpret the Scripture, we come to a much more pointed conclusion. The two witnesses are best fulfilled in the one image of the New Testament church. It is this same church that was born from the Old Testament prophecies, the nation of Israel, the giving of the Holy Spirit, and Jesus' sacrifice on Calvary. The Bible declares the two (Jew/Gentile and Israel/church) have become one.

At the same time, the two witnesses can be the restored and revived nation of Israel in the last days, since we are the only generation to ever experience this prophecy fulfillment, as well as the gospel-proclaiming church. And spiritually speaking, the two are standing before the world as one harmonious witness.

The following passage from Ephesians says almost everything presently stated. Note the highlighted portions specifically:

> Therefore, remember that formerly you who are Gentiles by birth and called "uncircumcised" by those who call themselves "the circumcision" (that done in the body by the hands of men)--remember that at that time you were separate from Christ, *excluded from citizenship in Israel* and foreigners to *the covenants of the promise*, without hope and without God in the world. *But now in Christ Jesus* you who once were far away have been brought near through the blood of Christ. For he himself is our peace, who *has made the two one* and has destroyed the barrier, the dividing wall of hostility, by abolishing in his flesh the law with its commandments and regulations. *His purpose was to create in himself one new man out of the two*, thus making peace, and in this one body to reconcile both of them to God through the cross, by which he put to death their hostility. He came and preached peace to you who were far away and peace to those who were near. For through him we both have access to the Father by one Spirit. Consequently, you are no longer foreigners and aliens, but fellow citizens with God's people and members of God's household, *built on the foundation of the apostles and prophets, with Christ Jesus himself as the chief cornerstone. In him the whole building is joined together and rises to become a holy temple in the Lord.* And in him you too are being built together to become a dwelling in which God lives by his Spirit.
>
> —EPH. 2:11–22 NIV; *emphasis added*

And do not forget, from our study in an earlier chapter in this book, that Paul had a revelation vision *before* John did! Paul would, more than likely, have known about the *two witnesses* of which John would ultimately speak in Revelation 11. Could it be that this is why Paul spent so much time punctuating that Jew and Gentile (the two men) have become one witness (one man) in Jesus Christ?

It has long amazed me how certain Bible scholars have no problem interpreting Zechariah's two witnesses as Israel and the church (or some similar scenario), yet when they arrive at the same imagery in Revelation, they give it an entirely new interpretation. And they do so in spite of the fact that the New Testament itself clearly defines both the olive tree and the lampstand within its own text. Consequently, when we *begin* our quest for understanding by first letting the Bible interpret the Bible, we often arrive closer to the truth.

THE TWO WITNESSES WERE BORN ON THE SAME DAY!

Another often-overlooked fact is that to this day the Orthodox Jews celebrate Shavu'ot (Pentecost) as the day commemorating the giving of the law at Mount Sinai. At the giving of the law to Moses and the children of Israel, the new nation of Israel was "born." This was the day on which God separated the Israelites from all other people on the earth. It would be through this nation that God would bring forth the witness of the Word of God, the prophets and prophecies of God, and ultimately—the Christ of God. On this day, Pentecost, the witness of Israel was born. It must also be noted that at the time of the giving of the law at Sinai, three thousand people were slain by the Lord for abject disobedience (see Exodus 32:28).

Of course, it was also on this same day (Pentecost), about fifteen hundred years later, that the witness of the church was born (see Acts 2). It was on this day that the first gospel sermon was proclaimed by the newly born witness, and the first converts-in-mass were born into the kingdom of God because of the witness of the gospel and the giving of the Holy Spirit. And it just so happens that on this day, three thousand new souls were added to the kingdom! God certainly keeps accurate books, does He not?

The nation of Israel, God's witness to the world of the coming Christ, was born on Pentecost through the giving of the law. The spirit-filled church, God's witness to the world of Jesus Christ, was born on Pentecost through the giving of the Holy Spirit. The two witnesses of God are now one.

Truly, this is the *only* definition the biblical text plainly gives us for the two witnesses. The two witnesses are the olive tree and the lampstand (see Rev. 11:3–4). Of that fact there can be no dispute. This is what, and *all*, the Bible specifically says in the matter.

This understanding of the two witnesses will be especially important in our upcoming examination of the seventh trumpet of Revelation because, as you will discover, it is at the blowing of the seventh trumpet that the witnesses are called up to heaven with a shout and a trumpet blast—into the clouds (see 1 Thess. 4:16). Sound familiar?

Let us now look at the trumpet visions of Revelation and their possible fulfillments within our lifetime. My own biblical expedition began with an amazing "third-trumpet" surprise.

14

SURPRISES

Society is always taken by surprise at any new example of common sense.

—RALPH WALDO EMERSON

The thirty-three-year-old preacher enthusiastically approached his pulpit and instructed his congregation to open their Bibles to the book of Revelation. The year was 1989.

For several weeks he had been preaching through that grand and mysterious apocalyptic book of the Bible. On this particular Sunday morning, he entered the specific section of Revelation dealing with the visions of the seven trumpets.

Even though the young pastor had no access to the Internet, or even a home computer (not readily available until the mid 1990s), he announced to his wide-eyed congregation that he *did* remember an article in a regional newspaper that said many people throughout Ukraine and Russia were identifying the 1986 Chernobyl nuclear disaster as the fulfillment of the wormwood prophecy of Revelation 8. The congregation let out a collective gasp of surprise. A few people nodded their heads; they had read the same article.

In fact, he announced, the referenced news article had specifically identified the English word *wormwood* as being synonymous with the word *chernobyl* in the Slavic languages.

As sensational as this sounded to the preacher and his hungry-for-the-Word congregation, he cautioned his audience: "Although this is startling information, and sounds very plausible, I haven't yet discovered a legitimate way to verify the report. I can't speak Ukrainian, nor do I know anyone who can."

The congregation laughed.

"Additionally," the pastor added, "I don't have access to a Ukrainian Bible so that I might verify that where our word *wormwood* is in Revelation 8, the word *chernobyl* is in the Ukrainian Bible. But wouldn't it be an absolutely amazing thing if that were so?"

Again there was laughter, mixed with a chorus of amens and nods of approval.

"However," he continued, "if this newspaper information *is* reliable, it could be the beginning of the confirmation of that which I have believed for many years—namely, the trumpet visions of Revelation may be speaking to our specific time of history. If this is so, and trumpet number three has already blown in the Chernobyl nuclear disaster, then common sense would *have* to dictate that trumpets one and two have *already* blown—and the prophetic *last days*, foretold in the Word of God, are well under way."

Now the expressions on the congregants' faces grew more somber. The preacher had them thinking. Of course, common sense *would* dictate the preacher's proposed conclusion if—and that is *if*—the third trumpet of Revelation was, in fact, the Chernobyl nuclear disaster.

The pastor continued, "If *wormwood* does not mean *Chernobyl*, then obviously there will be nothing to this line of reasoning. But if the two words *are* synonymous, we have a monumental possibility on our hands. Now," he said, "let's examine this possibility together . . ."

Years later, that young preacher would again make his preaching cycle through the book of Revelation. Once more, he would approach John's trumpet visions in his study and sermon preparation. Only this time, through the new technology of worldwide Internet search engines, he would gaze firsthand upon the heavily documented testimonies of native Slavic-speaking people—from Ukraine and Russia.

The preacher dug through the millions of Internet files until he found a Ukrainian Bible translation—and then ultimately, a Ukrainian dictionary. With trembling fingers and reserved anticipation, he hammered away at the computer keyboard, entering the words of Revelation 8:11, given to John on the island of Patmos, two thousand years earlier. And there, before his own eyes, he saw it . . .

***

I am that preacher. Because many years have now passed, I am no longer that *young* preacher. However, at the writing of this book, I am still the pastor of that same congregation. I arrived at Hickory Hammock Baptist Church in Milton, Florida, to be its senior pastor, in March 1987. I have since preached through the book of Revelation from my own pulpit several times. I have compiled stacks of sourced and heavily referenced research, much of it presented in this book. I have preached this information in several prophecy conferences around the world as the congregants listened, stunned. I have been checked and rechecked by amazed listeners seeking to verify what was presented.

It is an excellent thing to try to maintain a teachable and open spirit in this matter. We are treading on holy ground. We have a responsibility to be as accurate as is humanly possible when proclaiming the Word of God to others, especially in matters of potential prophetic fulfillment of scripture within our own lifetime.

At the same time, we would be remiss in our responsibility as faithful students of the Word if we did not at least explore the various possibilities of prophetic fulfillment as the news of the day unfolds before our eyes. This is called *being able to discern the times in which we live.*

Jesus had something to say about this to the religious leaders of His day who had failed to do that very thing: "When evening comes, you say, 'It will be fair weather, for the sky is red,' and in the morning, 'Today it will be stormy, for the sky is red and overcast.' You know how to interpret the appearance of the sky," He scolded, "but you cannot interpret the signs of the times" (Matt. 16:2–3 NIV).

No minister wants to hear a similar rebuke of their ministry from the Lord of glory. We would be foolish to refuse to examine what is happening in the world around us simply because it does not line up with a popular, and relatively modern, method of interpreting eschatology.

It does not matter how prepared, studied, sourced, and referenced your material may be—when you venture outside of your audience's (or peers') comfort zone, you tread on difficult ground. Sometimes you are openly rebuked. In the digital information age in which we now live, your maligned name may appear on a blog . . . and the unrelenting derision can be posted before the eyes of the world *forever.*

Consequently, a large number of preachers simply opt out of prophetic preaching, teaching, and exploration. And Satan is happy about it. He knows his time is short. But it was early in my ministry, with the reading of that newspaper article about Chernobyl and wormwood, when I really began digging into the Scriptures and modern historical news events.

Once I had considered the possibility that trumpet three might have already "blown," I went back and began to examine trumpet two, and then trumpet one. This made sense to me since, if trumpet three had indeed blown in 1986 with the Chernobyl disaster, then obviously trumpets two and one must have come to fruition sometime before 1986. Once I discovered the striking possibilities of the modern fulfillments of those two trumpets, I continued my examination with trumpets four, five, six, and seven. Accordingly, it is in this same investigative order of my initial study of these Revelation trumpet visions that I will present my findings in the remaining chapters of this book.

Are you ready to be surprised? Read on.

15

GONE ARE THE SOUNDS OF LIFE (TRUMPET 3)

We have also arranged things so that almost no one understands science
and technology. This is a prescription for disaster. We might get away with
it for a while, but sooner or later this combustible mixture of ignorance
and power is going to blow up in our faces.

—CARL SAGAN[1]

The disaster began during a routine test of the system. The day
was Saturday, April 26, 1986. It was 1:23 in the morning.
Reactor number four of the Chernobyl nuclear plant was
experiencing unexpected technical difficulties. The Chernobyl facility is near the city of Pripyat, Ukraine—close to
the Dnieper River.

In the early hours of the morning, there had been a sudden
power surge in the reactor. When an emergency shutdown was
attempted, an exponentially larger power spike took place. The
spiked output of energy led to a reactor vessel rupture and an

uncontrollable series of steam explosions. These horrifying and successive occurrences exposed the graphite core of the reactor to oxygen, causing it to immediately burst into flames.

The resulting explosion blew off the mammoth roof, scattering the insides of the reactor in a huge radius around the outside of the building, and igniting a raging fire in what was left of the graphite core. The blaze sent a deadly and fiery plume of highly radioactive fallout and chunks of the roof, mixed with other debris, over half a mile into the atmosphere, falling back to earth in a hellish, radioactive rain of rubbish.

The poisonous mass quickly spread over an extensive geographical area, including the neighboring Pripyat. The nuclear cloud continued to drift over large parts of the western Soviet Union and Europe. In the ensuing years more than 350,400 people would have to be evacuated. Within the next three months, thirty-one reactor workers and firefighters had died as a direct result of their exposure to the fallout. Soon thousands more would die.

Almost criminally, Soviet officials waited a full two weeks before giving an accounting of the matter to its citizens and then, finally, to the world. Tragically, no one was left more uninformed of the magnitude of the disaster than the Soviet citizens themselves.

At first, life continued as customary in Pripyat. The town had originally been constructed for the sole purpose of housing power station staff and their families. The town was located only one mile from the Chernobyl plant and contained 50,000 people.

Most of Pripyat's citizens spent the Saturday of the accident outside, enjoying the unusually beautiful spring weather. Children began playing and splashing in the large puddles of water standing in the roads. The children were unknowingly and haphazardly splashing radioactive material all over themselves.

Eventually, city workers began to distribute iodine tablets to the woefully uniformed, but speculative and gossiping, citizens. Some drank vodka as an added precaution, as the cultural superstition was that vodka could neutralize the effects of exposure to radiation.

Many rushed home to close their windows, hoping to keep the radiation out of their houses.

In a radio broadcast early the next morning, Pripyat officials announced that there had been an accident, and the town would be evacuated. That day eleven hundred buses from across Ukraine lined up in Pripyat. By 5 p.m., the city was empty. The surrounding villages were not informed or evacuated for several more days.

In Kiev, only a few miles away, citizens went ahead with their May Day parade, almost a week after the accident. They were completely unaware of the radiation that was quickly settling down upon them. No one had told them.

Today, in Pripyat, weeds have overtaken everything. The sports complex and the swimming pool are now empty and covered in debris. A rusted Ferris wheel turns in the wind—groaning and creaking as it slowly grinds away. It had been built just in time for May Day 1986.

The city's cultural center—once a place of dances, concerts, and other public events—stands desolate and lifeless. Trees are pushing up through cracks in the pavement. Numerous locations in the town still set off Geiger counters. The wind blows—but that is all. Gone are the sounds of life and laughter. All is silent.

Decades later, the city of Slavutych, a city built as a replacement for the citizens of Pripyat, held a midnight vigil in remembrance of the Chernobyl nightmare. Slavutych was constructed thirty miles from Chernobyl. It was designed to house the employees who continued, for the next fourteen years, to operate the remaining three Chernobyl reactors until they could finally be stopped in 2000.

In the center of Slavutych's town square is a black marble monument. The names of Chernobyl's first victims are etched on the marker. It was here that the frigid midnight service took place. The people lit candles and set wreaths under the monument. A priest and choir sang the mournful words of the accompanying dirge—"My God, my God, my God . . ."

More than 350,000 people evacuated the surrounding area after the Chernobyl disaster. Today, nearly 400 elderly residents have returned to their former homes to live out their lives. The ground is contaminated—but it is familiar. So, they have come back. It is here where they have willingly elected to live—*and to die.*[2]

16

THE NAME OF THE STAR WAS WORMWOOD (TRUMPET 3)

And the second angel sounded, and there fell a great star from heaven, burning as it were a lamp, and it fell upon the third part of the rivers, and upon the fountains of waters; and the name of the star is called Wormwood.

—REVELATION 8:10–11a

On September 16, 1997, eleven years after the Chernobyl nuclear disaster, Hennadiy Udovenko, minister of foreign affairs of Ukraine, gave his inaugural address as president of the fifty-second session of the General Assembly of the United Nations. The ninth paragraph of that speech reads as follows:

The current environmental problems also demand our increased attention. The sustainability of the entire ecosystem is put in question by the irresponsible exploitation of nature and by mismanagement. This poses a serious threat to our common well-being. The sad illustration of this is the Chernobyl catastrophe. It happened on the territory of my country, where—rephrasing the revelation of St. John the Divine—"a great star fell from heaven upon the third part of the rivers." Although it occurred more than a decade ago, the "Chernobyl star of Wormwood" still hovers like a Damoclean sword over the world and as a bitter reminder for all of us.[1]

Damocles, in classical mythology, was a courtier in the court of the Sicilian tyrant Dionysius II, or so the tale goes. Damocles so incessantly praised the powerful Dionysius that the despot, to show the precariousness of those with great rank and power, gave a banquet and suspended a sword—by a single hair—above the head of Damocles. From that came the expression "the sword of Damocles" to mean "an ever-present peril."[2]

On Mr. Udovenko's official United Nations biographical page, the former national representative is presented as a highly educated and extremely honored gentleman of distinction who is respected by his peers. According to his bio, the late Mr. Udovenko spoke fluent English, Russian, Polish, and some French.[3]

Before being appointed to the post of Ukraine's minister of foreign affairs, Udovenko was Ukraine's ambassador to Poland, from 1992 to 1994. He also held the diplomatic rank of ambassador extraordinary and plenipotentiary. A career diplomat, Mr. Udovenko worked for many years in the service of his country and for the United Nations, both in New York and in Geneva.[4]

Why would a man of Mr. Udovenko's distinction be so bold as to draw a definitive comparison between the Chernobyl, Ukraine, nuclear disaster of April 16, 1986, and the prophecy of the third trumpet of Revelation? Why would he feel so comfortable in making this politically incorrect and highly controversial statement in, of all places, his inaugural address as president of the United Nations General Assembly? He would say such a thing because he was confidently mindful of the history of the matter as well as the language of the Bible—especially as it is written in the Ukrainian tongue.

Surprisingly, this was not the first United Nations diplomat to speak to the similarities of the biblical prophecy of Revelation's third trumpet with the Chernobyl disaster. Chernobyl's biblical implications were clearly proclaimed seven years earlier in another conference at the United Nations.

A WORD FROM BYELORUSSIAN MINISTER PYOTR KRAVCHANKA

The following excerpts were translated from the Russian language to English and were reproduced in the official transcripts of the United Nations. The transcripts document the forty-fifth session of the UN General Assembly. They come from the excerpts of the provisional verbatim record of the thirty-second meeting held at Headquarters, New York, on Tuesday, October, 23, 1990.

Pyotr K. Kravchanka, minister of foreign affairs of the Republic of Belarus, spoke the ominous words:

> The fears Chernobyl caused for the future of nuclear power in the minds of its advocates are no justification for the lack of information available to the world community about the true scale of the Chernobyl disaster. . . .
>
> A mere glance at these charts will make it clear to you how unprecedented the situation in Byelorussia is in its complexity. Seventy per cent of the Chernobyl radionuclides landed on Byelorussia. They have contaminated a third of its territory. One in five of the total population, 2,200,000 people, including almost 800,000 children, have become the innocent victims of Chernobyl, hostages to the hazardous aftermath of radiation. From 120,000 to 150,000 people residing in zones of especially high risk are awaiting relocation to settlements now under construction in uncontaminated areas. The geographical limits and the safety criteria for living in the contaminated parts of the Republic have yet to be precisely defined. Over 30,000 people were evacuated in the very first months after the Chernobyl catastrophe. This area is now a radiation desert, depopulated no-go areas covering many hundreds of thousands of hectares, fenced off

with barbed wire. It will be impossible to live there for hundreds of years to come, even according to the most optimistic estimates. New patches of radiation contamination keep appearing. Decontamination is not producing the results we hoped for. Radionuclides are spreading throughout the Republic and are threatening to spread even beyond. They have been detected in people even in uncontaminated areas. . . .

Then there was this new ordeal: Chernobyl, the Calvary of the twentieth century for the Byelorussian people. As I stand at this rostrum, in my mind I can hear the now stilled voices of my people cry out over and over again the same question: Why? Why?[5]

Now consider as Mr. Kravchanka explains (in the same speech) the meaning of the biblical word *wormwood* from the vantage point of his own native language:

In Slavic languages, including the Ukrainian and Byelorussian languages, there is a word "chernobyl," which means wormwood, bitter grass. This has striking relevance to the Chernobyl tragedy. I am no fatalist. I do not believe in the blind inevitability of fate, but who can fail to be moved by these tragic and elegiac words from Revelation, which must leave their indelible imprint on the heart: ". . . and there fell a great star from heaven, burning as it were a lamp, and it fell upon the third part of the rivers, and upon the fountains of water; and the name of the star is called Wormwood: and the third part of the waters became wormwood; and many men died of the waters, because they were made bitter." (Rev. 8:10–11)[6]

By 1990, several startling truths had been recorded in the official records of the United Nations General Assembly—words spoken by a distinguished ambassador to the United Nations from Byelorussia. These words clearly explained that the English word *wormwood* was actually the Russian and Ukrainian word *chernobyl*. Furthermore, this same United Nations dignitary made the direct connection of the Chernobyl nuclear disaster of 1986 to the words of the third trumpet warning of the biblical book of Revelation. He made this connection without apology or equivocation.

However, these were not the only astonishing words spoken that day by Mr. Kravchanka. Observe the following declarations, particularly the words I have italicized:

A second Chernobyl must be prevented. We need the full store of international experience in the struggle against the consequences of such disasters. Such experience could be useful for the international community since *the Chernobyl disaster has global consequences.* This was shown in the report of the Scientific Committee on the Effects of Atomic Radiation published in 1988 and compiled on the basis of data provided by 34 countries. . . .

Let us hope that it will not be the words quoted above that great literary monument of all times and peoples, the Bible, that will be prophetic and prove to be our fate but rather the words of our national Byelorussian poet, Ouladzimir Dubouka, ringing with faith in the indomitable will, steadfastness and tremendous vitality of our people:

"Oh, Belarus, my wild rose,

A green leaf, a red flower

Neither whirlwind will ever bind you

Nor *chernobyl* [wormwood]* will ever cover"

Our people believe and trust that people of good will, fellow residents of our common home, planet Earth, will not leave us to face catastrophe alone.[7]

***

Sadly, a full twenty-five years after the Chernobyl disaster, Mr. Kravchanka's worst fears were not alleviated. Observe the first paragraphs from this article from the National Cancer Institute at the National Institutes of Health written in 2011:

---

*The bracketed word [wormwood] appears in the official transcripts exactly as reproduced above.

Nearly 25 years after the accident at the Chernobyl nuclear power plant in Ukraine, exposure to radioactive iodine-131 (I-131, a radioactive isotope) from fallout may be responsible for thyroid cancers that are still occurring among people who lived in the Chernobyl area and were children or adolescents at the time of the accident, researchers say.

An international team of researchers led by the National Cancer Institute (NCI), part of the National Institutes of Health found a clear dose-response relationship, in which higher absorption of radiation from I-131 led to an increased risk for thyroid cancer that has not seemed to diminish over time.[8]

Unknown to many Americans is the shocking fact that the Chernobyl disaster had direct links to thyroid cancer rates in the United States. Observe the following quote from an article titled "A post-Chernobyl rise in thyroid cancer in Connecticut, USA."

Recent analyses of children in Belarus and the Ukraine are the first to document large numbers of excess thyroid cancer cases only four years after exposure to radiation. In Connecticut (USA), a thyroid cancer increase of a much smaller magnitude occurred in 1990–93, 4-7 years after the Chernobyl accident, for both children and adults. Similar changes also occurred in the states of Iowa and Utah, which like Connecticut were exposed to low levels of radio-nuclides from Chernobyl fallout during May and June of 1986.[9]

Consider the following words from an article published in 2009 by the New York Eye and Ear Infirmary. The article speaks of the dramatic rise in thyroid cancer rates in the United States, and then elucidates the prominent effects that Chernobyl had on the United States—especially in the arena of immigration:

Thyroid cancer is one of a few cancers on the rise in this country over the past 20 years. In fact, your chances of getting thyroid cancer increased more than 3-fold during this time, and unlike many others, thyroid cancer affects a much younger population, more commonly women.[10]

Scientists still don't know for sure what causes this rapid rise in cancer rates. To most New Yorkers, the meltdown at the Chernobyl power plant in Ukraine on April 26, 1986, the greatest peacetime nuclear accident ever, is no more than a long-forgotten history lesson. Not so, however, to the hundreds of thousands of immigrants from that region now living in New York.

Chernobyl remains a horror story, a tale of governmental neglect and corruption, an accident that even now results in increased risk of thyroid cancer. You will see and hear this immigrant group on the streets of New York. In fact, Russian is the third most common foreign language spoken by New Yorkers, after Spanish and Chinese. HIAS (Hebrew Immigrant Aid Society), an organization that helped bring many of these immigrants to the United States from the then Soviet Union, estimated that more than 250,000 people exposed to radiation during Chernobyl came to New York after 1986 with its help. Another 100,000 to 150,000 Chernobyl victims came after the breakup of the Soviet Union.

While the immigrants to New York are able to enjoy all of the benefits this country has to offer, they still cannot escape the past—the effects of radiation exposure after Chernobyl are now being felt. And unfortunately, *thyroid cancer is now on the rise among all people exposed to radiation after Chernobyl, and rates are climbing.*[11]

As late as October 2014, Norwegian news sources were reporting that more radioactivity levels in grazing animals had been measured than in the almost thirty years before the Chernobyl explosion. Lavrans Skuterud, a scientist at the Norwegian Radiation Protection Authority, stated the matter in simple terms: "This year is extreme." Skuterud went on to explain that more than likely the extreme rise in radioactive levels was due in part to the unusually high amount of edible mushroom growth this year. The mushrooms, he explained, are especially susceptible to absorbing radioactivity in the soil, due to the Chernobyl disaster, and are eaten by both grazing animals and humans. The Norwegian reindeer seem to be the most affected of the tested animals thus far.[12]

The striking nature of the Chernobyl disaster and the tragic consequences of the event cannot be denied. Neither can it be denied that several influential and knowledgeable people have made an authoritative connection between that ominous event and the mournful words of the Revelation prophecy of wormwood.

The question that remains in the minds of many who are following and analyzing these events is, can we be certain the biblical word *wormwood* is synonymous with the Slavic word *chernobyl?*

In the next chapter, we will do a detailed study of this interesting word connection. And we will answer the question definitively.

.

17

A MERE GAME OF WORDS?
(TRUMPET 3)

Street names and birth dates and middle names, all kind of superfluous things appear related to each other. It's a ripple effect. So, what does it mean? Well . . . it means something's going to happen. Something big. But then, something's always about to happen.

—GRANT MAZZY, *in Pontypool*[1]

There is no shortage of books, articles, and blogs that hint that drawing a connection between the words *chernobyl* and *wormwood* is merely a nefarious ploy by those wishing to force a biblical link between them. Take, for example, this article, provocatively titled "Did your Christian Leaders ever tell you made up stories at church in order to keep you faithful?":

Back in the days when I was still a Christian, I was once taught in a service that the 1986 Chernobyl disaster was mentioned in the book of Revelation:

"And the third angel sounded, and there fell a great star from heaven, burning as it were a lamp, and it fell upon the third part of the rivers, and upon the fountains of waters; and the name of the star is called Wormwood: and the third part of the waters became wormwood; and many men died of the waters, because they were made bitter."

This was astounding biblical prophecy! We were told that Chernobyl translated into English means "Wormwood." And I went on believing this amazing prophecy for ages afterwards.

Except it doesn't mean that at all.

Translated to English, Chernobyl means approximately "Dark coloured grass"

Some [*expletive deleted*] in a church somewhere lied deliberately to us to create that story!

Recently I heard it spoken of again by a Christian on here [the Internet] and I was astonished that this nonsense story was STILL doing the rounds 20 years later![2]

At first glance this author appears to make a convincing argument. There are many similar objections in print and on the Internet. In fact, some articles go to exceedingly great lengths to explain away any biblical connections whatsoever between Revelation 8 and the Chernobyl disaster of 1986. After all, if there *is* a definitive correlation, then there is a very real possibility the Bible *is* the infallible Word of God. And even more startling is the implication that we could well be living in the trumpet days of Revelation.

Accordingly, this Internet critic has concluded that a direct name correlation between *chernobyl* and *wormwood* (especially of Revelation 8) is merely a church trick to keep you faithful. Notice, he begins the article by announcing that he no longer is a Christian. One can understand why this writer might prefer that an authoritative word connection not be made. However, he is mistaken in his conclusion, as I will soon demonstrate.

Consider another honest inquirer's posting on an online messaging board. It seems this inquisitive individual did a fair amount of research, but eventually became thoroughly confused. (Admittedly, the issue *can* be confusing when one considers that we are dealing with a Greek to English to Latin to Ukrainian/Russian translation of biblical words).

> I have seen in numerous places on the web the claim that Chernobyl is Ukrainian for "Wormwood." This would be significant because of Revelation 8:10–11's reference to a star named Wormwood falling to Earth and poisoning a third of the waters. Most of the web pages citing this as fact are, unsurprisingly, Christian fundamentalist websites, and I, having a base and suspicious mind, am not inclined to give much credit to Christian fundamentalist websites. On the other hand, I also found one non-fundie site which refers to the Chernobyl=Wormwood claim as fact. Now, a Ukrainian-English dictionary I found on the web has an entry for "wormwood," and none of what comes up looks anything like "Chernobyl" (or "Chornobyl" in Ukrainian). Aha! I say. Another stupid fundie urban legend. (Which suckered in a few secular types as well.) But then, a little further research turns up a number of official references to a "Project Polyn" in connection with the aftermath of the Chernobyl disaster. And Polyn does mean "wormwood" according to the Ukrainian-English dictionary above. Furthermore, this site from the University of Hawaii, which appears to be a translation of an official document from the Kurchatov Institute, states that "POLYN" is a Russian word and means "Chernobyl." So at this point I don't know what to think.
> . . . Any of the 9,315 of you speak Ukrainian (or have a grandmother who does)?[3]

For the record, there are also serious and publicly professing Christians who question the word associations. One Catholic apologist blogger claimed that "'Chernobyl' is the name of a plant, but it isn't wormwood. It's mugwort." He claimed that a Russian author got the two plants confused when he was speaking with the New York Times, which is where the rumor started. The blogger said that technically the name for chernobyl in Ukranian is *polyn hirkyj*, "which means 'bitter polyn' or 'bitter artemis.' . . . so if a Ukrainian speaker wants to refer to mugwort, he'll say 'chornobyl' but if he wants to refer to wormwood, he'll say 'polyn.'"[4]

It appears that the gentleman who wrote this was genuinely attempting to provide a reputable service to the Christian community. I applaud his efforts to that end. However, let us now register factual responses to his assertions. First of all, it is a matter of fact that native speakers of the Slavic languages would disagree with him on the common Ukrainian reader's *natural* association of the words *chernobyl* and *wormwood*.

One of the blogger's sources was an article from Wikipedia. It is my understanding that for years Wikipedia and Snopes (a self-proclaimed urban-legend-debunking website) claimed it was just an urban myth that *wormwood* translated to *chernobyl* in Slavic languages. I personally accessed the Wikipedia article that made this claim some years back. That particular reference is no longer available. As a matter of fact, as of this writing, I am unable to find either of these debunking articles. Actually, Wikipedia now has something quite different to say about the word associations in question. We will get to those entries in a moment.

The author of the aforementioned article makes a reference to a "Russian author speaking to the New York Times" who "got the word associations wrong." However, my research has been unable to confirm the fact that any reputable Russian speaker has yet to "get wrong" the word associations between *chernobyl* and *wormwood*—but more on that in a moment.

Let us consider a more detailed answer to the critics by recalling the United Nations speeches from the previous chapter. Both of the speakers, Mr. Pyotr K. Kravchanka, minister of foreign affairs of the Republic of Belarus, and Mr. Hennadiy Udovenko, minister of foreign affairs of Ukraine, intimated that the word *chernobyl* has definitive connections to the English word *wormwood*. Recall that Mr. Udovenko drew the correlation by stating, "The 'Chernobyl star of Wormwood' still hovers like a Damoclean sword over the world and as a bitter reminder to us all." Notice that he also used the imagery of a "bitter" reminder as a means of further drawing the connection between the words *chernobyl* and *wormwood*. The word *bitter* is connected to the definitions of both of the words *chernobyl* and *wormwood*.

Mr. Kravchanka stated, "In Slavic languages, including the Ukrainian and Byelorussian languages, there is a word 'chernobyl,' which *means* wormwood, bitter grass. This has striking relevance to the Chernobyl tragedy."

It would seem to be a reasonable consideration that these two men, both representing their countries as UN dignitaries, would have been relatively certain of the remarkable word connections before using them in speeches of this nature.

But let me elucidate further the connection between these words. Author Mary Mycio identifies herself as a visitor to the Chernobyl site some ten years after the horrific disaster. She has written of her experience with her native-born Ukrainian guide, Rimma Kyselytsia, in a book titled *Wormwood Forest: A Natural History of Chernobyl*. As the author's guide is showing her around Chernobyl, she crouches down and points out a short bush growing out of a crack in the concrete. The bush is described as about a foot tall, with small cottony flowers growing out from the the purplish stems. Ms. Mycio then describes how her guide crushed one of the leaves and offered it to her in order to smell of its "varnishy aroma." When the author asked her guide what the plant was she replied, "Chernobyl." Ms. Mycio goes on to explain that *chernobyl* with an "e" is the Russian-ized version of the Ukrainian word *chornobyl*.

Ms. Mycio says she was accompanied on her trip by Svitlana, whom she identifies as her botanist companion. Svitlana explained to Ms. Mycio that chornobyl is actually *Artemisia vulgaris*, while wormwood is *Artemisia absinthium*. The Ukrainian common name, she expounded, is polyn. The botanist went on to explain, "Botani-cally and chemically, *Absinthium vulgaris* is so similar to *A. absin-thium* that *A. vulgaris* is also sometimes called 'wormwood,' though 'mugwort' is a more common English name. In Ukrainian, as well, *polyn* and *chornobyl* are sometimes used synonymously."[5]

Also consider the following statement from *The Chernobyl Disaster* by Viktor Haynes: "Chernobyl is a Russian transliteration of the Ukrainian word 'chornobyl,' which in English means wormwood, a perennial plant."[6] According to Mr. Haynes' biography, he was "born in the Ukraine during the Second World War."[7] It is a safe bet that a Ukrainian-born native speaker of the language and distinguished author on the topic of the Chernobyl disaster would be intimately familiar with his own language and the nuances of the word associations of that language.

Interestingly, on the same page where Haynes explains the origin of the word *chernobyl*, he also quotes Revelation 8:10–11—thus directly tying the word to the prophecy of Revelation's third trumpet, as did Hennadiy Udovenko in the earlier cited UN speech.

Now consider these words from a *New York Times* article published in July 1986, only three months after the Chernobyl accident:

MOSCOW, July 25— A prominent Russian writer recently produced a tattered old Bible and with a practiced hand turned to Revelations [*sic*]. "Listen," he said, "this is incredible: 'And the third angel sounded, and there fell a great star from heaven, burning as it were a lamp, and it fell upon the third part of the rivers, and upon the fountains of waters; and the name of the star is called wormwood: and the third part of the waters became wormwood; and many men died of the waters, because they were made bitter.'"

In a dictionary, he showed the Ukrainian word for wormwood, a bitter wild herb used as a tonic in rural Russia: *chernobyl*.

The writer, an atheist, was hardly alone in pointing out the apocalyptic reference to the star called *chernobyl*.[8]

In the enormous depth of my research in this matter, this is the only *New York Times* article I could find in which a Russian author speaks of the word associations that are in question. Now, it may very well be that this article is the same one to which our earlier blogger referred when he wrote of a "Russian author speaking to the *New York Times*" who got the word associations "confused" and started "the rumor" that the plant chernobyl was wormwood.[9] However, this specific article makes no mention of the Russian author "getting it wrong" or "confusing" the two words. It does say that with "uncanny speed" his "discovery" spread throughout Russia in "rumor" fashion, but that assessment does not mean that his word associations were incorrect. Furthermore, the article does not say that this Russian's "discovery" was disputed anywhere in his country by native Russian or Ukrainian speakers.

Consider yet another example of the connection between wormwood and Chernobyl by native speakers of the Slavic languages. This quote is from a Boston University study titled "The Russian Idea of Apocalypse":

> During my initial visits to the Chernobyl region in 1990–91, on the eve of the fifth anniversary of Chernobyl, I often would ask Belarusians: "Do you have a religious opinion about Chernobyl?" They typically answered "yes" and proceeded to rehearse the long history of suffering in Belarus. Frequently, they would cite the "Wormwood star" in the writings of the Bible as referring specifically to the 1986 Chernobyl disaster.
>
> In a 1994 national poll, 1,550 Belarusian citizens (including a quota sample of 244 institutional leaders) were asked a variety of questions, including how strongly they disagreed or agreed with the following statement: The Chernobyl disaster was prophesied in the Revelation of John and was therefore inevitable.
>
> . . . The surprisingly high number of "Agree" and "Strongly Agree" responses among certain segments of the population was considered significant.[10]

THE APPARENT TRUTH OF THE MATTER

Native Russian and Ukrainian speakers in various times and places have affirmed that *chernobyl* and *wormwood* are synonymous. Furthermore, they affirm that the words are often used interchangeably among Slavic-speaking people.

While, to me, the issue could be declared "settled" upon the word of these various native Slavic-language speakers alone, I do wish to verify the matter in one other manner. To many people, this can be a confusing topic from the outset—simply because so many languages and word associations are used.

In Revelation 8, the *Greek* word that is translated to English as *wormwood* is *apsinthos*, #894 in the *Strong's Greek Dictionary*. The definition in *Strong's* for *apsinthos* is: Of uncertain derivation; wormwood (as a type of bitterness, i.e. [figuratively] calamity).[11]

The Latin word for the wormwood plant is *Artemisia vulgaris. A. vulgaris* (mugwort or common wormwood) is one of several species in the genus *Artemisia* commonly known as mugwort, although *A. vulgaris* is the species most often called mugwort.[12]

Mugwort is called *chornobylnik* in Ukrainian, and has given its name to the abandoned city of Chernobyl (Chornobyl in Ukrainian).[13]

Note this encyclopedia entry concerning the city of Chernobyl and the etymology of that city's name:

> The city name is the same as a local Ukrainian name for *Artemisia vulgaris* (mugwort or common wormwood), which is also чорнобиль or "chornobyl."[2] An alternative etymology holds that it is a combination of the words *chornyi* (чорний, black) and *byllia* (билля, grass blades or stalks); hence it would literally mean black grass or black stalks.[14]

You will recall from the book *Wormwood Forest*, previously cited in this chapter, that the last sentence of the citation reads: "In Ukrainian . . . polyn and chornobyl are sometimes used synonymously." This is an important fact because the Ukrainian Bible cites Revelation 8:11 with these words: І ймення зірки тієї — «Полин» ("And the name of the star is called Полин").[15] Why is that significant?

---

[2] Gernot Katzer's Spice Pages, Mugwort (Artemisia vulgaris L.), by Gernot Katzer, 4 July 2006.

The Ukrainian word Полин is *polyn* (translated to English as *wormwood*) or synonymously . . . *chernobyl*. The Ukrainian translation of the Bible and the normal understanding of the Ukrainian language, and its various nuances, is precisely why the Slavic language experts cited in this chapter are on record equating the biblical word *wormwood* with the Ukrainian word *chernobyl*. This is also why they are on record making the connection between the Chernobyl nuclear disaster of 1986 with the ominous words of the prophecy of Revelation 8. To the Slavic mind, reading that passage of Scripture, one could easily read the portentous words of Revelation 8:11 as "And the name of the star was Chernobyl."

Is this indisputable revelation merely a coincidence of fate? How could John the Revelator have known that some disaster of worldwide magnitude would strike the future world—just before the time of the end—and that it would happen in a place that would identify the trumpet warning as *wormwood* . . . or *chernobyl*? There are only a few possible answers to these questions:

1. It is an utter coincidence—one in several million—but a coincidence nonetheless. But would God really allow such a coincidence to infect His Word only to confuse His people in the last-days generation and appear as some type of cruel and cosmic joke? Most likely not.

2. It is simply an error of word associations. However, it has been clearly demonstrated that this is not the case. There is no error in the mind of those who speak the Slavic languages.

3. It is exactly what it appears to be: a biblical trumpet warning to the people of God living in the time of the biblical last days.

If the third one is the answer . . . then we have some more thinking to do. And we have more questions to ask.

18

CHERNOBYL: WAS IT A SIGNIFICANT WORLD EVENT? (TRUMPET 3)

And it fell upon the third part of the rivers, and upon the fountains of waters; and the name of the star is called Wormwood:
and the third part of the waters became wormwood; and many
men died of the waters, because they were made bitter.

—REVELATION 8:10b–11

The word *wormwood* appears seven times in the Old Testament (there's that number *seven* again!). Each time, it is used in reference to *judgment* or *calamity*. It is mentioned only twice in the New Testament, both times in Revelation 8:10–11. Obviously, it is used there as an image of bitterness, judgment, and disaster.

The fraction *one-third*, or "the third part" (found several times in the Revelation trumpet visions), is an interesting designation. What exactly does it mean? Does it mean a literal one-third of something, or is it a figure of speech meant to point to the overall magnitude of the event in question? The Lord is certainly capable of determining the literal number of a thing. However, I do not believe it is absolutely necessary to hold to a literal number for the prophecy to have powerful meaning and a direct fulfillment in an observed earthly calamity.

Think of the fraction *one-third*. What is *one-third* of something? Clearly, *three-thirds* of a thing would be the entire thing . . . the *whole* of it. *Two-thirds* of a thing would be the obvious majority of something—but not *all* of it. On the other hand, *one-third* of something would not be all of it, or even the majority of it, yet it would be a significant amount of something—significant enough that in the case of a *trumpet event* most of the world would have to notice it. In other words, it would be a calamity on a monumental scale—a judgment of which the *last-days world*, to which the trumpet warning was directed, would have to take note. Many believe this understanding is, at least, what the number *one-third* means in the trumpet prophecies of Revelation. The designation *one-third* is used frequently throughout the trumpet prophecies, so it would prove beneficial to us to give this designation some serious consideration.

Now let us consider the profoundness of the Chernobyl disaster. How big was it on a *theater* scale . . . and how big was it on a global scale? Let us examine some leading journalistic and scientific assessments of that question. You can be the judge. Was Chernobyl a *one-third* prophetic event?

AN EVENT OF GLOBAL PROPORTIONS?

In 2007, a full twenty-one years after the Chernobyl explosion, *Time* ran a special online article announcing its list of the world's most polluted places. Of all the places listed, Chernobyl, Ukraine, was named as the worst in the world in terms of the most people affected, potentially for decades to come. *Time* magazine put the initial number of people impacted at 5.5 million. Observe the ominous words of this assessment—over two decades after the accident:

When Chernobyl melted down on Apr. 26, 1986, the ruined plant released *100 times more radiation into the air than the fallout from the nuclear bombs at Hiroshima and Nagasaki.* Today the 19-mi (30-km) exclusion zone around the plant remains uninhabitable, and between 1992 and 2002 more than 4,000 cases of thyroid cancer . . . were diagnosed among Russian, Ukrainian and Belarusian children living in the fallout zone. *"It's the largest industrial accident in the world,"* says [Richard] Fuller [of the Blacksmith Institute]. *"It'll be contaminated for tens of thousands of years."* Fortunately, work is being done to prevent further radiation spill from the ruined sarcophagus of the nuclear plant.[1]

Following are more examples of the gravity of the Chernobyl (wormwood) disaster. Considering what you will read in the next several pages, there should be no doubt left as to the *one-third* magnitude of this event, thus qualifying it as a prime candidate for the fulfillment of the third-trumpet prophecy of Revelation.

This next quote is from a Russian Academy of Sciences article titled "Atmospheric, water, and soil contamination after Chernobyl," published in 2009, twenty-three years after the Chernobyl nuclear plant exploded:

Air particulate activity *over all of the Northern Hemisphere* reached its *highest levels* since the termination of nuclear weapons testing—sometimes up to *1 million times higher than before the Chernobyl contamination.*

There were *essential changes in the ionic, aerosol, and gas structure of the surface air* in the heavily contaminated territories, as measured by electroconductivity and air radiolysis.

Many years after the catastrophe aerosols from forest fires have dispersed hundreds of kilometers away.[2]

Consider the following statement from an article in *National Geographic* written in October 2013:

The fallout, 400 times more radioactivity than was released at Hiroshima, drove a third of a million people from their homes and triggered an epidemic of thyroid cancer in children. Over the years, the economic losses—health and cleanup costs, compensation, lost productivity—have mounted into the hundreds of billions of dollars. As evidence of government bungling and secrecy emerged in its wake, Chernobyl (or Chornobyl, as it is now known in independent Ukraine) even sped the breakup of the Soviet Union.[3]

A March 2011 article in *Scientific American* told readers that the Chernobyl explosion "sent plumes of reactive dust as far away as Japan" and the United States.[4]

Next is an excerpt from a book by Bernard L. Cohen, professor emeritus at the University of Pittsburgh. In a chapter titled "The Chernobyl Accident—Can It Happen Here?" Cohen wrote:

For the first two days after the accident, the winds carried the radioactive dust over Finland and Sweden. On the third and fourth day, the wind shifted to bring it toward Poland, Czechoslovakia, Austria, and Northern Italy. It then shifted further southward to deposit the material over Rumania and Bulgaria. *People all over the world were exposed* to external radiation from radioactive gases and dust suspended in the air and settled on the ground. Some of the material on the ground will continue to be radioactive for many years, exposing people externally and internally through the food supply. The estimated average total exposure in millirems after the first year will be 120 in southeastern Europe, 95 in North and Central Europe, 81 in the USSR, 15 to 19 in Western Europe and Southwest Asia, 8 in North Africa, and less than 2 elsewhere (0.4 in North America). *The sum of exposures to people all over the world* will eventually, after about 50 years, reach 60 billion mrem, enough to cause about 16,000 deaths.[5]

In other words, . . . Chernobyl had *world-reaching consequences*.

Next we will observe the overall environmental impact of the Chernobyl disaster as represented in a scientific article published by GreenFacts.org, whose stated mission is "to bring the factual content of complex scientific consensus reports on health and the environment to the reach of non-specialists." Concerning the excerpt that follows, GreenFacts states: "This Digest is a faithful summary of the leading scientific consensus report produced in 2006 [twenty years after the accident] by the UN Chernobyl Forum: 'Chernobyl's legacy: Health, Environmental and Socio-Economic Impacts.'" Observe what this report declares to be the leading scientific consensus:

> The Chernobyl accident is *the most serious accident in the history of the nuclear industry.* Indeed, the explosion that occurred on 26 April 1986 in one of the reactors of the nuclear power plant, and the consequent fires that lasted for 10 days, led to *huge amounts of radioactive materials* being released into the environment and a radioactive cloud *spreading over much of Europe.* The greatest contamination occurred around the reactor in areas that are now part of Belarus, Russia, and Ukraine. . . .
>
> *At present, more than five million people live in areas that are considered to be "contaminated"* with radioactive materials from the Chernobyl accident. . . .
>
> Regarding agriculture, the contamination of crops, meat, and milk with short-lived radioactive iodine was a major concern in the early months after the accident. Now and *for decades to come,* contamination with longer-lived radioactive caesium is the main concern in some rural areas. . . .
>
> The high transfer of radioactive caesium from lichen to reindeer and from reindeer meat to humans has been demonstrated after the Chernobyl accident in the *Arctic and sub-Arctic areas of Europe.* The accident led to high contamination of reindeer meat in Finland, Norway, Russia and Sweden and caused significant problems for the indigenous Sami people.[6]

It becomes obvious, with a minimal amount of research, that the Chernobyl disaster affected far more than simply the Chernobyl area and the immediately surrounding environ.

Consider also the following report from a 2006 article, titled "UN accused of igorning 500,000 Chernobyl deaths," in the UK's *Guardian*:

> United Nations nuclear and health watchdogs have ignored evidence of deaths, cancers, mutations and other conditions after the Chernobyl accident, leading scientists and doctors have claimed in the run-up to the nuclear disaster's 20th anniversary next month.
>
> In a series of reports about to be published, they will suggest that at least 30,000 people are expected to die of cancers linked directly to severe radiation exposure in 1986 and up to 500,000 people may have already died as a result of *the world's worst environmental catastrophe.*[7]

BUT WHAT ABOUT THE WATER?

One of the most striking features of the wormwood prophecy is the mention of the poisoning of the water supply and the people who died from that poisoning. What does the scientific and journalistic community have to say about water contamination from Chernobyl?

Two years after the Chernobyl explosion, the UK *Independent* reported:

> SCIENTISTS monitoring the shelter encasing the ruins of the Chernobyl meltdown have detected signs that it is leaking highly *radioactive water capable eventually of causing a "catastrophe" by poisoning the water supply* of Ukraine, a country the size of France.
>
> Tests on bore holes around the giant sarcophagus that encloses the remains of Reactor 4, which exploded in 1986 causing the worst nuclear disaster in history, have detected signs of thritium, a radioactive isotope of hydrogen, *in subsoil water.*
>
> This has raised fears that it could eventually find its way into the nearby Dneiper River, or into the water table, and—after many years—*into the drinking water* of Ukraine's 50 million population.[8]

In Pulitzer Prize–winning author Richard Rhodes's book *Arsenals of Folly*, the third volume in his history of nuclear weaponry, Rhodes gives a vivid description of the Chernobyl blast. Rhodes states that radioactive blocks and pieces of graphite crashed to the ground all around the building. Some of the debris fell into the four-mile-long cooling pond that lay between the Chernobyl plant and the Pripyat River. The river eventually drained into a large reservoir that stored the water supply of Kiev, a city of about 2.5 million people and Russia's third-largest city.[9]

Here is the scientific assessment by three Russian scientists from a report twenty-three years after the accident:

> The Chernobyl radionuclides concentrate in sediments, water, plants, and animals, sometimes 100,000 times more than the local background level. *The consequences of such a shock on aquatic ecosystems is largely unclear.* Secondary contamination of freshwater ecosystems occurs as a result of Cs-137 and Sr-90 washout by the high waters of spring. The speed of vertical migration of different radionuclides in floodplains, lowland moors, peat bogs, etc., is about 2-4 cm/year. As a result of this vertical migration of radionuclides in soil, plants with deep root systems absorb them and carry the ones that are buried to the surface again. This transfer is one of the important mechanisms, observed in recent years, that leads to increased doses of internal irradiation among people in the contaminated territories.[10]

One might ask, "Is water contamination limited merely to Chernobyl and the immediately surrounding area?" Again, we will consult the scientific community for our answer. The following information comes from a 2000 issue of the scientific journal *Nature*:

> Radiocaesium (137Cs) from the 1986 Chernobyl accident has *persisted in freshwater fish in a Scandinavian lake for much longer than was expected.* On the basis of new data generalizing this observation, we propose that the continuing mobility of 137Cs in the environment is due to the so-called "fixation" process of

radiocaesium in the soil tending towards a reversible steady state. Our results enable the contamination of foodstuffs by Chernobyl fallout to be predicted over the coming decades. *Restrictions in the United Kingdom, for example, may need to be retained for a further 10–15 years—more than 100 times longer than originally estimated.*[11]

The United Nations Scientific Committee on the Effects of Atomic Radiation (UNSCEAR) estimates there has been a collective *global dose of radiation* exposure from the Chernobyl nuclear accident "equivalent on average to 21 additional days of world exposure to natural background radiation." In other words, on average, every man, woman, boy, and girl around the world has now been exposed to the equivalent of twenty-one straight days more radiation than they would normally have received from so-called background radiation. However, UNSCEAR also reports that 530,000 local Chernobyl-area recovery workers averaged an effective dose equivalent to an *extra fifty years* of typical background radiation.[12]

WHAT ABOUT THE SARCOPHAGUS?

Following the Chernobyl disaster in reactor number four, a hasty project commenced to encase the radioactive facility in a concrete enclosure, or *sarcophagus*. The designing of the concrete enclosure box started on May 20, 1986. Construction of the massive shroud lasted 206 days. Once completed, the sarcophagus locked in 200 tons of radioactive corium, 30 tons of highly contaminated dust, and 16 tons of uranium and plutonium—enough radiation to kill 50 million people.[13]

Today, after all these years, there still remains a strong presence of viable radioactive material at reactor four. And the steel structure that was built to contain the material is on the verge of collapsing. It is the "fire that can't be put out," says Alexei Okeanov of the International Sakharov Environmental University in Minsk, Belarus.[14]

The steel structure was "built in six months" and was supposed to last only twenty years. The "fragile shelter holds an estimated 200 tons of nuclear fuel"—enough enriched uranium and plutonium for dozens of bombs. Scientists believe the risks are minimal but "a renewed chain reaction could trigger another steam explosion, blowing open the sarcophagus, scattering chunks of fuel, and releasing tons of fine radioactive dust."[15]

On the twenty-fifth anniversary of the disaster, Scientific American published an article on the Chernobyl disaster. There we read these portentous words concerning the precarious sarcophagus:

> "It was really quite a remarkable feat, but after 25 years, it's in danger of collapse," civil and environmental engineer Eric Schmieman of Battelle Memorial Institute explains in an interview in Kiev.
>
> The sarcophagus, technically known as the Shelter Object, was made of more than 7,000 metric tons of metal and 400,000 cubic meters of concrete. It was erected as quickly as possible to limit worker exposure to radiation, and was never meant to last forever. In many ways it was designed "like a house of cards," Schmieman says, with pieces of metal essentially leaning against each other and hooked together. "There are no welded joints or bolted joints—it wouldn't take much of a seismic event to knock it down."[16]

It would appear the Chernobyl disaster is not a finished story—but one that continues to unfold, perhaps with more disastrous consequences just around the corner.

"BUT JOHN SAID HE SAW A *STAR* FALLING FROM HEAVEN . . ."

And the third angel sounded, and there fell a great star from heaven, burning as it were a lamp.

—REV. 8:10

This is a common objection to the notion that the 1986 Chernobyl disaster could be the event that John described. After all, the detractors would say, Chernobyl involved no "star"—and nothing fell from *heaven*. Certainly, we can understand these objections, but there is so much more to consider before we simply dismiss the matter.

First, John was thrust at least two thousand years into the future. There can be no denying this fact. Since this is the case, could it be that what he saw was not an actual *star* but rather something that *looked like* a star to him? Perhaps the word *star* was the only word he could give to the amazing spectacle.

Also note that the word for *heaven* used in this text is the Greek word *ouranos* (*Strong's Greek Dictionary* #3772), primarily used to denote the *sky.* The word can be used to specify the domain of God's particular *heaven,* but it certainly does not have to be.

We use the word *heaven* in a similar manner in the English language. For example, I might say to you, "Even though the world is in turmoil, God is in His heaven" (God's abode). Or, I might look into the night sky and proclaim, "Wow! Look at the beauty of the heavens!" (the moon and stars). Additionally, I could say, "The birds are filling the heavens with their glory this morning!" (the lower atmosphere). I just used the same word three different ways. The interpretation of the word depends upon the context of usage.

Consider this possible scenario: John is in the Spirit and propelled into the future—to the year 1986. Remember, John was still living in the days of oil lamps and camel travel. It could be that he was taken, in the Spirit of prophecy, to the site of a nuclear reactor in a faraway city that did not yet exist—and he was confronted with an unimaginable power-technology that would not exist for thousands of years. John may have witnessed a massive nuclear catastrophe . . . and the resulting horrendous spectacle of it all. Briefly and cryptically, John recorded what he saw. By the Spirit of God, what if he was given the name of the *star*, or the *place*, or the *city*, or the *event* . . . and what if he was told what he had witnessed was called *Chernobyl* (if the Slavic language was to be used)?

"But," one might object, "nothing fell from the sky on that fateful night. How could that part of the prophecy fit what actually happened at Chernobyl?"

The truth of the matter is vividly described in Richard Rhodes's book *Arsenals of Folly*. Rhodes describes how the graphite core of the mammoth concrete-encased reactor was an enclosed cylinder forty feet in diameter and twenty-three feet tall. He describes the lid of the structure as a "two-million pound, disk-shaped upper biological shield of concrete blocks."

The first explosion, Rhodes explains, lifted the two-million-pound lid. Then the second and most powerful explosion "tilted the lid up almost vertical." With that second blast, the upper half of the reactor core was shattered. It then blew several tons of molten radioactive debris through the roof and "half a mile into the air." After the second explosion, Rhodes describes the debris as raining back down on the facility's roofs and setting them ablaze.[17]

It is a scientific fact that an actual *star* is virtually a giant nuclear reactor.[18] Chernobyl exploded over half a mile into the sky and fell back to earth, literally "burning [like] a lamp" (Rev. 8:10). The disaster was made worse because it rained all over Europe after the accident, thus, according to many reports, dumping nuclear fallout into the surrounding European water supply.

What if this was the same event John witnessed in his vision of the future? What if this is what he was told to describe with the only words he had at the time? How would *you* have described such a terrifying event not slated to happen until two thousand years later?

Considering the preceding information, we are left with only a few logical possibilities with regard to the third trumpet of Revelation and the Chernobyl disaster:

1. Any possible relation between them is just a startling and mathematically improbable coincidence;

2. There have been errors in interpreting the information; or

3. Chernobyl was the precise fulfillment of what John saw.

These are important considerations, because practically everything that follows in this book hinges on the answer. If it is the third option, then there is a distinct possibility we are now living in the *trumpet days* of Revelation. Not surprisingly, many around the world believe this to be a clear-cut fulfillment of a prophetic *trumpet warning*.

19

WARS AND RUMORS OF WARS (TRUMPET 2)

I can still picture them in my mind—like walking ghosts.
—Survivor of the Hiroshima nuclear blast [1]

f the third trumpet of the wormwood prophecy was actually fulfilled in 1986, then it stands to reason the first two trumpet warnings of Revelation would have blown sometime *before* the Chernobyl nuclear disaster. If this is so, what could these trumpet warnings possibly have been? In what unprecedented events could they have been fulfilled? Many believe the first potential clue is to observe the *key words* found in the trumpet number two declaration:

> The second angel sounded his trumpet, and *something like a huge mountain, all ablaze, was thrown into the sea.* A third of the sea turned into blood, a third of the living creatures in the sea died, and a third of the ships were destroyed.
>
> —REV. 8:8–9 NIV; *emphasis added*

This prophecy appears to describe an event of horrendous devastation. The calamity obviously involves a tremendous death toll as well as the destruction of a large number of maritime vessels. The event apparently happens in or near a large body of water.

Interestingly, the word translated into English as *sea* is the Greek word *thalassa.* This Greek word can mean the sea, as an ocean, and/or figuratively, as a vast expanse of a surface area, or a specific theater. Both Revelation 4:6 and 15:2 speak of a "sea of glass" before the throne of God. The Greek word *thalassa* is used in these specific verses as well. Obviously, the *sea* in these verses is not a literal ocean of water but rather *a vast expanse.*

The prophecy also speaks of the "living creatures" that died within this vast expanse. This specific Greek word could refer to actual marine life within a literal sea, and/or it could also refer to life in general, associated with the theater in which this specific prophecy would unfold. Regardless of how one approaches these matters, to numerous students of prophecy it seems the operative clue in interpreting this biblical foretelling undoubtedly is the "huge mountain—all ablaze."

Notice, though: John specifically says he saw something *like* a huge mountain. The word *like* is important. In other words, it was *not* a literal mountain thrown into the sea that John actually observed. John was attempting to describe something he had never seen before, and he had no words with which to describe the vision he had just watched. The closest thing to which he could compare what he saw was something that *resembled* a mountain being thrown into the sea—and the *mountain-thing* appeared to be on fire.

MOUNTAIN THROWN INTO THE SEA

There is only one event in history that remotely comes close to such a description—especially *before* 1986 (trumpet three). Many believe that John was shown the unprecedented nuclear bomb explosions over Japan, thus bringing World War II to its final and long-awaited end. The bombings of Hiroshima and Nagasaki were the first times in history that nuclear weapon technology was used, and with devastating results. The shock of that event reverberated throughout the world. To date, a nuclear attack of that proportion has never been duplicated.

On August 6, 1945, the United States deployed the world's first atomic weapon against Hiroshima, Japan. This nuclear bomb, nicknamed Little Boy, was the equivalent of twenty thousand tons of TNT. Once detonated, it completely flattened the city, killing tens of thousands of civilians. Three days later, while Japan was still trying to comprehend the desolation, the United States struck again, this time on the city of Nagasaki.

Few people have not seen the abundant pictures of those ominously fiery, voluminous mushroom clouds—appearing *out of the sea* over Japan. Who can imagine that a man living two thousand years ago, sitting on a rocky, prison-camp island, having been thrust into the future and shown this first nuclear event in world history—would *not* describe the event in precisely such a manner? Every time I make a personal presentation of this study and show a video clip of a nuclear explosion or the pictures of the Hiroshima bomb—people gasp. They clearly see *the huge mountain—all ablaze.* There is no mistaking the imagery.

And remember, Japan would have been unknown to John. Japan sits as an island in the *middle of the sea.* If John was shown this prophetic event and actually saw the gigantic, purple-red fiery mushroom cloud rising over forty thousand feet out of the sea (higher than the world's tallest mountain) and blooming over the island of Japan—it would not be a stretch of the imagination to accept his description of it as *something like a huge mountain, all ablaze.*

The Greek word John used for *huge* is *mega.* Interestingly, the word not only means "exceedingly great in size," but it also can mean "extraordinarily loud," as in our use of the English word *megaphone.* By using this word, John may not have merely been describing the size of the thing he saw, but also the deafening sound that emanated from it. By using *mega,* he may have been saying, "The fiery mountain was big and loud!"

Additionally, John said the fiery mountain was "thrown" into the sea. The Greek word chosen for the action of throwing is *ballo* (*Strong's* #906). The word has multiple meanings, one of them being "sent," or even "violently sent." Interestingly, the foremost translation of this Greek word into English is "arise." If translated this way, John would have said he saw "something like a huge mountain arising out of the sea." By using this particular Greek word, *ballo,* there is a sense in which the thing John saw was both *violently sent* (dropping of the bomb) and it *arose* (the atomic plume) out of the sea—almost simultaneously.

The atomic bomb Little Boy was created using uranium-235, a radioactive isotope of uranium. This uranium-235 atomic bomb, a product of $2 billion of research, had never been tested. Nor had any atomic bomb yet been dropped from a plane. Some scientists and politicians pushed for not warning Japan of the bombing, to save face in case the bomb malfunctioned.[2]

Let us take a closer look at this monumental and unparalleled nuclear event. Observe the following account:

> On August 6, 1945, the first choice target, Hiroshima, was having clear weather. At 8:15 a.m. (local time), the Enola Gay's door sprang open and dropped "Little Boy." The bomb exploded 1,900 feet above the city and only missed the target, the Aioi Bridge, by approximately 800 feet.
>
> Staff Sergeant George Caron, the tail gunner, described what he saw: "The mushroom cloud itself was a spectacular sight, a bubbling mass of purple-gray smoke and you could see it had a red core in it and everything was burning inside. It looked

like lava or molasses covering a whole city . . . It's like bubbling molasses down there . . . the mushroom is spreading out . . . fires are springing up everywhere . . . it's like a peep into hell." The cloud is estimated to have reached a height of 40,000 feet.[3]

Here's another glimpse, this time of the aftermath of the bombing—including the death toll:

Captain Robert Lewis, the co-pilot, stated, "Where we had seen a clear city two minutes before, we could no longer see the city. We could see smoke and fires creeping up the sides of the mountains." Two-thirds of Hiroshima was destroyed. Within three miles of the explosion, 60,000 of the 90,000 buildings were demolished. Clay roof tiles had melted together. Shadows had imprinted on buildings and other hard surfaces. Metal and stone had melted.
Unlike many other bombing raids, the goal for this raid had not been a military installation but rather an entire city. The atomic bomb that exploded over Hiroshima killed civilian women and children in addition to soldiers. Hiroshima's population has been estimated at 350,000; approximately 70,000 died immediately from the explosion and another 70,000 died from radiation within five years.[4]

Did you note the number of deaths that occurred in a five-year span? Roughly 140,000 out of 350,000—a little more than one-third of the entire population was decimated. There again is that prophetic number, *one-third*.

However, consider the entirety of this unparalleled war from which the calamitous use of nuclear technology emerged. You will remember from a previous chapter of this book, titled "Unprecedented" that almost seventy nations of the world were involved, directly or indirectly, in World War II. More than 100 million people from these various nations were directly engaged within fighting military units. It is frequently estimated that more than 200 million people may have been involved, including the civilians who worked to support the war effort directly. In a state of "total war," the major national powers threw their entire economic, industrial, and scientific resources behind the war effort. This unprecedented move virtually erased the distinction between most civilian and military assets.[5]

The number of deaths resulting from World War II has been estimated at about 60 million people. It just so happens that 60 million is approaching one-third of 200 million. Again, the number *one-third* shows up. Consider the following heart-wrenching words from a survivor of that horrific event:

> The appearance of people was . . . well, they all had skin blackened by burns. . . . They had no hair because their hair was burned, and at a glance you couldn't tell whether you were looking at them from in front or in back. . . . They held their arms bent [forward] like this . . . and their skin—not only on their hands, but on their faces and bodies too—hung down. . . . If there had been only one or two such people . . . perhaps I would not have had such a strong impression. But wherever I walked I met these people. . . . Many of them died along the road—I can still picture them in my mind—like walking ghosts.[6]

World War II commenced September 1, 1939, with Germany's invasion of Poland. On August 15, 1945, Japan surrendered. The surrender documents were finally signed aboard the deck of the American battleship USS *Missouri* on September 2, 1945.

World War II sparked off several additional unprecedented events that would play directly into future biblical prophecies. One of the most apparent results of the war was that the United States of America undeniably emerged as the world's foremost superpower. The international prominence of this superpower status resulted in the United States being thrust front and center into many skirmishes, lengthy wars, overseas nation-building efforts, uprisings, and civil wars the world over—a number of which involved the Middle East and its political/religious affairs.

Consequently, the United States eventually became the world's leading economic engine—literally driving the global economy and setting global currency standards. As a result, with these factors firmly entrenched, the office of the president of the United States became the most powerful office of leadership and global influence the world had ever seen. The power, the wealth, the influence, and the ability to effectively manipulate world affairs were *unprecedented*.

As a result of these unparalleled realms of influence, the United States of America was then able to wield its influence in helping reestablish the new nation of Israel. Many believe the reemergence of this ancient biblical nation to be a direct fulfillment of a twenty-five-hundred-year-old prophecy of monumental consequence.

Through the years the United States has been one of Israel's foremost allies and protectors—thus assuring Israel of a Middle Eastern superpower presence. Israel's presence and *assisted-superpower* status have been a thorn in the side of the surrounding Arab and Muslim nations ever since. This has been the source of most of the unrest in the Middle East and was actually declared by Osama bin Laden to be one of the major reasons for the al-Qaeda attacks on America on September 11, 2001.

Also, we must not forget that if this huge, fiery mountain of John's vision was the nuclear blast of World War II, it was with the dropping of these bombs that the nuclear age was born—for better or for worse. And with the birthing of this new technology, the nuclear reactor at Chernobyl could eventually be built. Consequently, with the building of this particular nuclear reactor—it is quite conceivable the fulfillment of trumpet number three was made possible.

All of this, and more, emerged from the shadows of World War II, a dreadfully unprecedented event. And of all things, World War II was finally brought to an end by the occurrence of something resembling *a huge mountain, all ablaze, thrown into the sea.*

20

SCORCHED EARTH
(TRUMPET 1)

The fear of death follows from the fear of life. A man who lives fully is prepared to die at any time.

—MARK TWAIN

Certainly, the image of fire and burning, and the ensuing massive destruction of that ominous ordeal, are set forth as the presenting clue in the first trumpet vision. What is it that John might have seen sometime before the atomic blast that ended World War II?

The first angel sounded his trumpet, and there came hail and fire mixed with blood, and it was hurled down upon the earth. A third of the earth was burned up, a third of the trees were burned up, and all the green grass was burned up.

—REV. 8:7 NIV

If trumpet three was the Chernobyl nuclear disaster (wormwood), and trumpet two was a description of the nuclear blast over Japan that ended World War II, then trumpet one occurred sometime before that unprecedented nuclear devastation.

ONE-THIRD OF THE ENTIRE EARTH?

Those who reject the idea that the trumpets of Revelation might be in the process of current fulfillment often point to the imagery in the first trumpet regarding one-third of the "earth" being burned up. The problem with this objection is that they are relying solely upon the English translation of the imagery and immediately assuming this word has to mean the entire globe. In actuality, the Greek word for *earth* in this passage allows for something much more local in nature.

The specific Greek word used in this passage is *geen* (*Strong's* #1093) and is defined as "soil; by extension a region, or the solid part of the globe, as well as the occupants of each."[1] In this context John could easily have been speaking of a specific theater—that is, a specific region—of prophecy fulfillment, rather than the entirety of the planet, when he used the word that we translate as *earth*. He would have been well within the proper usage of the word.

With this in mind, there appear to be two viable candidates of consideration for the first shofar blast. Both candidates, as we have already discovered, are unarguably linked in history. The first possibility is that the first trumpet might be a vision of the earliest days of World War II, and, specifically, an allusion to the infamous "scorched earth" tactic of warfare so prolifically and infamously employed in that particular war.

SCORCHED EARTH?

The *scorched earth policy* has been around for thousands of years. Some date the first known usage of the military tactic to the Scythian/Persian wars of the time of Darius the Great, of biblical fame. But there can be no doubt the most famous and most prolific use of this hideous warfare tactic was employed by Joseph Stalin against the German army in World War II.[2] So what is it, exactly?

The scorched earth policy is a military strategy whereby all of the assets that the enemy could possibly employ are targeted for utter destruction. The land, the citizens, crops, property, buildings, and supplies are *scorched*, often by literal burning, so that nothing usable remains. Certainly, the first trumpet vision foreshadows something of this magnitude.

Because this activity is so hideously inhumane, annihilating the food and sustenance supply of civilians living in a war zone, it has since been banned under Article 54 of Protocol I of the 1977 Geneva Conventions:

> It is prohibited to attack, destroy, remove, or render useless objects indispensable to the survival of the civilian population, such as foodstuffs, agricultural areas for the production of foodstuffs, crops, livestock, drinking water installations and supplies, and irrigation works, for the specific purpose of denying them for their sustenance value to the civilian population or to the adverse Party, whatever the motive, whether in order to starve out civilians, to cause them to move away, or for any other motive.[3]

Despite being banned, unfortunately, the scorched earth tactic is still a common military strategy. Prominent nations that have not yet ratified the protocol are the United States, Israel, Iran, and Pakistan.[4]

Therefore, some Bible prophecy experts see the first trumpet as the ominous sign of the beginning of the most destructive war in the history of humanity—marked by the famous *scorching of the earth*. They would then surmise that the *second* trumpet prophecy marks the end of that war with the dropping of the nuclear bombs over Japan. In other words, trumpets one and two make up the beginning and then, finally, the end of the largest and deadliest war in history. This scenario certainly makes sense and possesses biblical and historical credibility.

However, there is another legitimate consideration for the first-trumpet vision. Many believe it to be a vision John had of World War I.

WORLD WAR I

The First World War began in 1914 and ended in 1918. It is probably most famously called the Great War. World War I, as documented in the chapter titled "Unprecedented," has also been branded as unparalleled in history as far as the total amount of slaughter and destruction it caused. It was the first global war in human history, involving more than 65 million troops from at least thirty nations and claiming between 9 and 13 million lives. Nothing like it had ever happened before, and in fact, the only thing remotely like it since grew *out* of it, twenty-one years later: World War II.

The imagery of "hail and fire mixed with blood . . . hurled down upon the earth" seems to be another one of those horrible and indescribable scenes John was attempting to put into the only words he knew at the time. Numerous video clips of both World War I and World War II depict unimaginable fire and hail-like bullets and missiles being unleashed from the *heavens* (planes) and pelting the earth, bringing massive death and destruction. Fiery, morbid scenes of infernos, scorching of the earth and cities, and horrendous carnage marked World War I. To an ancient man sitting in a rock island prison camp, certainly scenes like this could be described as recorded in Revelation's first-trumpet vision.

Ironically, World War I was labeled in the popular colloquialism of the day "the war to end all wars," a designation taken from British author and social commentator H. G. Wells's book *The War That Will End War.*[5]

Initially, the United States, under the leadership of President Woodrow Wilson, stayed clear of the quickly intensifying world war. But in January 1917, the German foreign minister, in the now-famous Zimmermann Telegram, summoned Mexico to join the growing war efforts. Mexico was to play the role of Germany's ally against the United States of America. In return for Mexico's entry into the war and its cooperation with Germany, the Germans promised to finance Mexico's war efforts and to assist Mexico in recovering the territories of Texas, New Mexico, and Arizona.[6]

Britain intercepted the message outlining the plot against the United States and presented the telegram to the U.S. embassy. From there, the note was given to President Wilson. The president released the Zimmerman note to the American public. Americans saw it as a just cause for entering the war. President Wilson called on various antiwar elements *to end all wars* by winning this one and eliminating militarism from the globe.[7] After Germany's sinking of seven US merchant ships by submarines, and the mass publication of the Zimmerman Telegram, President Wilson called for war on Germany. The United States Congress declared war and thus entered the Great War on April 6, 1917.

Because of the apparent lack of a definitive *key word* in the first-trumpet narrative, it is a little more difficult to pinpoint a particular fulfillment—although the two candidates just presented appear to be highly plausible. Regardless, the key words *wormwood* and *a huge mountain all ablaze* in trumpets two and three find noticeable possibilities of fulfillment in the Chernobyl disaster and in World War II, respectively. Because of the connections between these striking clues in the Revelation trumpet visions, and their possible alignment with documented historical events, many Bible students of today are convinced the first trumpet vision that John saw was connected to World War I or the beginning of World War II. Accordingly, numerous students of the Bible are certain the trumpet days of Revelation have been upon us since the early 1900s.

In trumpets four and five, however, we find even more striking correlations with recent historical events, especially the breathtaking connections of trumpet five. The next two chapters will set forth those links.

Be prepared for some shocking discoveries.

21

WHO TURNED OUT THE LIGHTS? (TRUMPET 4)

I really didn't believe it . . . I thought there was some error in the apparatus.
—DR. GERALD STANHILL, *The Israeli Agriculture Ministry*[1]

n the fourth trumpet, there are no names given, no places identified, and no specific identifying factors elucidated. There is, however, that number *one-third* again. It would thus appear that this trumpet is significant and perhaps serves as a time marker, of sorts.

The fourth angel sounded his trumpet, and a third of the sun was struck, a third of the moon, and a third of the stars, so that a third of them turned dark. A third of the day was without light, and also a third of the night.

—REV. 8:12 NIV

At first, it might look as if this prophecy of Revelation holds no particularly deep connections to significant historical events. But if we are really onto something, and if these trumpet prophecies actually do correlate with historical events of our lifetime, this trumpet would *have* to comply with the model of interpretation thus far.

Additionally, as you will see in the next chapter, the fifth trumpet prophecy is so chock-full of clues, with indisputable word associations connected to historical events, that if trumpet five has already occurred, then trumpet four *must* have occurred as well. Accordingly, we must ask ourselves, what *one-third event* has happened in relatively recent history that would bring this prophecy to life?

First, we must determine: what is the main message of the trumpet four announcement? It would appear to proclaim that something atmospheric will take place in the last days that affects the amount of light given off (or *received* on earth) by the heavenly bodies. This seems to be a reasonable and rather literal interpretation of the passage. But has anything like this ever occurred? Furthermore, has it occurred to the extent of dimming the heavenly bodies by *one-third?*

A STUNNING REVELATION

In May 2004, the *New York Times* published an article that startled the scientific community. It was titled "Globe Grows Darker as Sunshine Diminishes 10% to 37%." Please note the figure "37%." That's just a little more than *one-third.* Here is an excerpt from that article:

> In the second half of the 20th century, the world became, quite literally, a darker place.
>
> Defying expectation and easy explanation, hundreds of instruments around the world recorded a drop in sunshine reaching the surface of Earth, as much as 10 percent from the late 1950's to the early 90's, or 2 percent to 3 percent a decade. In some regions like Asia, the United States and Europe, the drop was even steeper. In Hong Kong, sunlight decreased 37 percent. . . .
>
> "There could be a big gorilla sitting on the dining table, and we didn't know about it," said Dr. Veerabhadran Ramanathan,

a professor of climate and atmospheric sciences at the University of California, San Diego. "There are many, many issues that it raises."

Dr. James E. Hansen, director of the NASA Goddard Institute for Space Studies in Manhattan, said that scientists had long known that pollution particles reflected some sunlight, but that they were now realizing the magnitude of the effect.

"It's occurred over a long time period,'" Dr. Hansen said. "So it's not something that, perhaps, jumps out at you as a person in the street. But it's a large effect." . . .

The dynamics of global dimming are not completely understood. Antarctica, which would be expected to have clean air, has also dimmed.

"In general, we don't really understand this thing that's going on," said Dr. Shabtai Cohen, a scientist in the Israeli Agriculture Ministry who has studied dimming for a decade. "And we don't have the whole story."

The measuring instrument, a radiometer, is simple. . . .

Since the 50's, hundreds of radiometers have been installed from the Arctic to Antarctica, dutifully recording sunshine. In the mid-80's, Dr. Atsumu Ohmura of the Swiss Federal Institute of Technology in Zurich sifted through the data to compare levels in different regions. "Suddenly,'" Dr. Ohmura said, "I realized it's not easy to do that, because the radiation was changing over time." . . .

At that time, Dr. Gerald Stanhill of the Israeli Agriculture Ministry noticed similar darkening in Israel.

"I really didn't believe it," Dr. Stanhill said. "I thought there was some error in the apparatus."[2]

Observe, also, the words of this report by the BBC in an article titled "Global Dimming":

We are all seeing rather less of the Sun. Scientists looking at five decades of sunlight measurements have reached the disturbing conclusion that the amount of solar energy reaching the Earth's surface has been gradually falling. Paradoxically, the decline in sunlight may mean that global warming is a far greater threat to society than previously thought.

The effect was first spotted by Gerry Stanhill, an English

scientist working in Israel. Comparing Israeli sunlight records from the 1950s with current ones, Stanhill was astonished to find a large fall in solar radiation. "There was a staggering 22% drop in the sunlight, and that really amazed me," he says.

Intrigued, he searched out records from all around the world, and found the same story almost everywhere he looked, with sunlight falling by 10% over the USA, nearly 30% in parts of the former Soviet Union, and even by 16% in parts of the British Isles. Although the effect varied greatly from place to place, overall the decline amounted to 1–2% globally per decade between the 1950s and the 1990s.

Gerry called the phenomenon global dimming, but his research, published in 2001, met with a skeptical response from other scientists. It was only recently, when his conclusions were confirmed by Australian scientists using a completely different method to estimate solar radiation, that climate scientists at last woke up to the reality of global dimming.[3]

It is interesting to note that much of the research and the discovery of facts concerning global dimming is centered on the nation of Israel.

Following is yet another attestation of the undeniable global dimming phenomenon as reported by *NOVA*:

Like enormous clouds of volcanic ash, some forms of air pollution can significantly reduce the amount of sunlight reaching Earth's surface and lower temperatures. Climate researcher James Hansen estimates that "global dimming" is cooling our planet by more than a degree Celsius (1.8°F) and fears that as we curb these types of air pollution, global warming may escalate to a point of no return. [4]

Readers are then invited to launch an interactive feature tracing the historic events that have led these scientists to their understanding of global dimming.

As late as May 2012, The *Guardian* (UK) ran an article confirming the reliability of the cataloging of this phenomenon. It reads, in part, "Measurements from the 1960s to the early 1990s, *backed up by a wide range of data and a number of independent studies,* showed there were substantial declines in the amount of the sun's energy reaching the Earth's surface. This reduction is known as 'global dimming.'"[5]

While numerous studies of late have breathlessly claimed that *global dimming* seems to be on the reverse, it cannot be denied that a phenomenon that scientists the world over were able to monitor and record, did occur. What's more, their data indicated that as much as *one-third* of the light coming to the earth was being dimmed! Some people believe the abundance of material now attempting to proclaim a *reverse* of global dimming is the direct result of the prominence that the new, politically correct (and financially lucrative) *global warming* claim has gained in the most recent years. The idea of global dimming (and subsequent cooling effect on the earth) goes against the more popular ideology of global warming—thus the possible attempts to minimize the global dimming phenomenon that has actually been scientifically observed, measured, and credibly demonstrated. But, could this monumental and scientifically documented phenomenon of global dimming account for what scientists are now claiming is a new worldwide cooling effect—or the newly coined phrase of global *climate change*? In May 2014, *American Thinker* published an article stating the following:

"With global temperature data now available for the first three months of 2014, an interesting trend has clearly emerged: global cooling. No longer is it just a hypothesis. For the first quarter of each calendar year since 2002, it is effectively a fact at reasonably strong statistical significance."[6]

It appears we now possess two pieces of hard-science evidence with definitive correlations: global dimming and global cooling. The two appear to go hand in hand.

Is the information you just read from BBC, *NOVA*, and the *Guardian* concerning *global dimming* the description of trumpet four? Is it mere coincidence that this two-thousand-year-old prophecy tells of a time near the end of days when the light received on the earth would be dimmed by as much as one-third—and in just the last couple of decades, credible research verifies that this exact phenomenon has indeed occurred? The global dimming data, to many, certainly appear to describe the prophecy—to an absolute T. While I am not prepared to rigidly declare, "This is that," I can say the evidence certainly is strong for the possibility of the fulfillment of trumpet four within our historical lifetime.

In light of the surprising details found in trumpet five (revealed in the next chapter), trumpet four's fulfillment in this globally recognized *light-dimming* phenomenon would not be a surprise to many who are diligently researching these matters.

Now let us move to the prophecy that appears to possess the mother lode of key words and clues. As dramatic as the third trumpet keys appear (wormwood, etc.), in the minds of many, trumpet five rivals that drama.

22

OPEN THE PITS! (TRUMPET 5)

The ugly, black, and threatening sky spread from horizon to horizon with midday as black as midnight.

—BERT HOUSTON, *war correspondent*[1]

The fifth trumpet vision may be the most striking of all the trumpet visions with respect to key words that are defined by examining relatively modern-day events. The correlations are extraordinary. They are so prominent, in fact, that they cause some prophecy researchers to do a double take.

Observe the words of the fifth trumpet vision of Revelation 9. I have emphasized those portions that may have documented correlations to events that have actually happened:

¹ The fifth angel sounded his trumpet, and I saw a star that had fallen from the sky to the earth. The star was given the key to *the shaft of the Abyss.*

² When he opened the Abyss, *smoke rose from it like the smoke from a gigantic furnace. The sun and sky were darkened by the smoke from the Abyss.*

³ And out of the smoke locusts came down upon the earth and were given power like that of scorpions of the earth.

⁴ They were told not to harm the grass of the earth or any plant or tree, but only those people who did not have the seal of God on their foreheads.

⁵ They were not given power to kill them, but only to torture them *for five months.* And the agony they suffered was like that of the sting of a scorpion when it strikes a man.

⁶ During those days men will seek death, but will not find it; they will long to die, but death will elude them.

⁷ The locusts looked like horses prepared for battle. On their heads they wore something like crowns of gold, and their faces resembled human faces.

⁸ Their hair was like women's hair, and their teeth were like lions' teeth.

⁹ They had breastplates like breastplates of iron, and the sound of their wings was like the thundering of many horses and chariots rushing into battle.

¹⁰ They had tails and stings like scorpions, and in their tails they had power to torment people *for five months.*

¹¹ *They had as king over them the angel of the Abyss, whose name in Hebrew is Abaddon, and in Greek, Apollyon.*

—REV. 9: 1–11 NIV, *emphasis added*

Notice that the clue of *five months* is repeated twice in this prophecy. We are also told that this five-month period resulted in the dramatic darkening of the skies, even in the middle of the day, over this particular theater of prophecy fulfillment. And we learn that the *king* who caused this event has a definitive name—a name we are able to research, and even define. These factors are hugely important.

Here, in the fifth trumpet, the name of a person is given to us: Abaddon, or Apollyon. Certainly, other striking information is given as well. We will examine those additional details a little later on.

The events and the details described next are highly documented. The only thing left to do, after this examination, is to ask ourselves: Are these correlations mere coincidences, or are they the precise fulfillments of biblical prophecy?

UNPRECEDENTED

It is a fact that Saddam Hussein invaded Kuwait on August 2, 1990. It is also a fact that the United States of America finally engaged the Iraqi forces in Kuwait on January 16–17, 1991—*five months later*, to alleviate the death, terror, and destruction being suffered by the Kuwaiti people (it was on January 16 in the United States and on January 17 in Kuwait).[2]

Verse 5 of this prophecy states the tormentors were not given the power to "kill" the people—only to torment, or to torture them. The Greek word used here for *kill* is *apokteino* (*Strong's Greek Dictionary* #615). Obviously, its primary meaning is simply "to kill." But when used figuratively, it means "to utterly destroy," which fits the Saddam scenario precisely. Iraq did not "utterly destroy" Kuwait, but rather it tormented them, as the prophecy says, for exactly five months.

Additionally, it is well documented that, as a part of Saddam's *scorched earth policy* of warfare, he set almost eight hundred oil wells on fire, hemorrhaging more than six million barrels of oil a day.[3] This massive amount of oil going up in smoke, each and every day, was much more than Kuwait's normal daily production and considerably more than Japan's daily oil imports. The scale of this inferno was so much larger than anything even the most practiced oil well firefighting firms had ever experienced. It was an unprecedented event. A host of new oil well firefighting techniques had to be quickly developed.[4]

The fires burned, the hellish smoke filled the air, and the sky turned to blackness in the middle of the day for a period of almost ten solid months. The sun and moon were, often, literally blotted from view. Many of the first fires were set in January 1991; the last oil well was not extinguished until November 1991.[5]

THE ABYSS

There is another shocking word study in this passage. The English translation of the trumpet five prophecy mentions the word *abyss*. Most of us understand the imagery when this particular word is used. It invokes a scene of a foreboding, hellish environment. This is exactly the way many of the eyewitnesses of this unparalleled event described the scene.

However, there is another startling revelation about this particular word: the English word abyss comes from the Greek word *abussos* (*Strong's* #12). The word *abussos* means "bottomless." But, in the original Greek translation the word abyss is coupled with the word pit (as in "bottomless pit"). The Greek word for pit is *phrear* (*Strong's* #5421). The word *phrear* can be translated as a "pit," "a hole in the ground," or "a prison." However, the primary translation, according to Strong's, is "a well."

Unbelievably, this passage of Scripture appears to inform us that a certain event would take place involving five months of suffering and torment for a specific people. A part of the suffering could be interpreted to involve something defined as a well with furnace-like fire and smoke emanating from it, the result of which would be the blocking out of the sun and the moon.

The Revelation description in the fifth trumpet pictures terror and ghastly destruction. Observe this report, which came directly out of the days of Iraq's invasion of Kuwait and the subsequent oil well fires set by the retreating Iraqi troops:

> Hussein's soldiers left Kuwait burning. Almost eight hundred oil wells were set aflame, with temperatures as high as three thousand degrees, creating a hellish mixture of fire and darkness and choking smoke and gross environmental damage. As much as six million barrels of oil a day were going up in flames.[6]

Additionally, consider this report from *People* magazine, written within weeks of the fires originally being set. The article is titled "Fields of Fire":

> Up close, the burning Kuwait oil well *seems like some sort of cyclone from hell*: a 40-foot wall of bright red, orange and yellow flames that erupts from the earth like a 747 at takeoff. . . . With the gouting flames, smoke and noise, the scene is *nothing short of infernal.*
>
> "You half expect to see *little guys with pitchforks and tails* coming out of the ground," says Dave Wilson, an engineer. To add to the confusion, Saddam's demolition experts blew up each well differently, creating individual puzzles. Meanwhile, another 50 to 100 wells that did not catch fire have turned into runaway geysers of oil, forming *oleaginous black lakes.*[7]

Observe this next amazing description of the bleakness and the darkness. It speaks of an ominous, almost spiritual, blotting out of the sun. The article is titled "Noon Is Black as Midnight," by war correspondent Bert Houston:

> The shadow of Saddam Hussein left over Kuwait after his army was smashed by allied forces has given local soldiers who were embroiled in the conflict, a chilling vision they will never forget . . . a black, eerie scene which could have come straight from the pen of a science fiction writer describing the height of a nuclear winter. The TV pictures and even the eye-witness accounts of the dark, boiling smoke pouring into the skies from the oil wells set afire by the defeated Iraqis could never prepare anyone to awake to the morning *the sky dawned black.* The servicemen and women had accepted as normal the choking fumes and ugly drifting palls of smoke Rising into the skies and leaving behind *a darkened day* as its clouds spiraled out to the gulf.
>
> But the full horror of exactly what these fumes could do began to show when the wind dropped. In conditions without a breath of air, the oily leaden clouds built up overnight until, even 50 miles into the desert, *dawn was simply blotted out.*

The ugly, black and threatening sky spread from horizon to horizon with *midday as black as midnight—so black that a torch had to be used to read the time on a wrist watch.* It was as if a frightening nightmare had come true. With *the sun blotted out,* the air was bitter and soldiers hurried to put on their warmest clothing in the desert. Two Dumfries soldiers I spoke to were shaken and stunned—it seemed so unbelievable.[8]

It would certainly appear, if we really are looking at John's fifth trumpet vision, that John picked the perfect word to describe the scenario. By choosing the Greek word *phrear* he depicted both a *well* and a scene of fiery hellishness unleashing nightmarish effects upon the people—both of which existed in Kuwait in 1991. Of course, twentieth-century technology would have been entirely foreign to him. How could he adequately describe it with the limited words he had and the ancient technology of the AD 90s?

Yet, as we pull the words apart more than two thousand years later, it seems in the minds of many that John *nailed* the scene—as we now know it.

However, perhaps the most startling clue of all is the name that John gave to the man or entity at the center of the entire calamitous affair—*Abaddon.*

23

THE DESTROYER COMETH
(TRUMPET 5)

It was as if a frightening nightmare had come true.

—BERT HOUSTON, *war correspondent*[1]

Without a doubt, the most remarkable of all the correlations regarding the coded words in the fifth trumpet revelation of John are aligned with the very last words of the prophecy:

They had as king over them the angel of the Abyss, whose name in Hebrew is Abaddon, and in Greek, Apollyon.

—REV. 9:11 NIV

Here we are given the *name* of the entity that causes this entire event to commence. It seems this Abaddon, or Apollyon, is the central figure of, and ultimately responsible for, the complete mess of which we read in the fifth trumpet prophecy. So, who could this be?

The words *Abaddon* (Hebrew) and *Apollyon* (Greek) translate to the "destroyer."[2] The Bible calls this individual "the angel of the Abyss." The Greek word for *angel* is *Strong's #32, aggelos*, which simply means "messenger." As such, this entity does not have to be a literal heavenly being from the spiritual dimension. The idea being conveyed here is that the one named Abaddon, the focus of this terrible event, is the *messenger* of destruction.

Accordingly, the person in question would appear to be known as one who is bent on destruction—perhaps even known by the very title "the Destroyer." But let's be real. What are the chances this prophecy could have anything to do with something familiar to *our* time?

According to an article published in *Slate* magazine in November 1998, titled "What's the Name of Saddam Hussein?": "Saddam Hussein has no family name. Rather 'Hussein' is the name his parents gave the nascent dictator, and 'Saddam' is an epithet he adopted before he grabbed power, and is derived from the Persian word meaning, 'crush.' 'Saddam Hussein' is best translated as Hussein-Who-Crushes-Obstacles or Hussein-*the-Destroyer*."[3]

However, there is still more confirmation of this amazing correlation between Saddam Hussein and the *Abaddon* of Revelation 9. Peter Beaumont, of the UK's *Observer*, wrote, "So why is it that so many Iraqis, even those who suffered most seriously at his hands, remain so ambivalent about the process against Saddam, whom they nicknamed *The Destroyer?*"[4] Even the Iraqis know that his name means "The Destroyer," which, again, in Hebrew is Abaddon!

But there were others who thought they were seeing a possible fulfillment of Revelation trumpet prophecies in the Saddam-initiated Gulf War. Ministers of the various strains of the Christian faith saw the connection. A United Pentecostal preacher and founder of a prominent end-time ministry relates that a particular edition of the *German Tribune* contained an article on the Gulf War in which Saddam Hussein was referred to as Saddam "the destroyer" Hussein. The same minister tells of reading a particular human-interest story in a copy of the *Jerusalem Post Weekly International Edition* wherein a Jewish woman, escaping Baghdad with her family, told the story of Saddam Hussein's birth. The minister quotes the article, "When he was finally born, his mother decided to name him Saddam, since he had caused her so much pain." The article, the minister says, declares the name Saddam means "the destroyer."[5]

It also is apparent that even Saddam Hussein's enemies knew exactly what his name meant, and openly spoke of its meaning. Consider this tirade leveled against Saddam by Muslim cleric Muqtada al-Sadr, as reported by the Associated Press in November 2003: "There is no enemy of Iraq but Saddam the destroyer and his cronies, whom we denounce until judgment day and they are in immortal hell."[6]

As if the preceding information were not enough to confirm a correlation between Abaddon and Saddam, a telling PBS interview in October 2001 with Laurie Mylroie sheds a bit more light on the subject. Mylroie is the author of two books on Saddam Hussein. Her most recent book, *Study of Revenge—Saddam Hussein's Unfinished War Against America*, constructs an evidentiary case that "Saddam was behind the bomb plot to topple the World Trade Center towers in 1993 and that two Iraqi intelligence agents were masterminds of the plot." Here's a portion of the transcript (emphasis added):

> **PBS:** You had a conversation with General Wafiq al Samarrai, who helped define the reason why—after all the pressure of UNSCOM, the U.N. weapons inspection team sent into Iraq—they would not give up this weaponry. Help us define the Iraqis' view of these weapons.

MYLROIE: General Samarrai was head of the Iraqi intelligence. He defected in late 1994 to the Iraqi National Congress, and I spoke with him in the fall of 1995 after Hussein Kamal's defection. Samarrai told me at that point that Iraq was terribly dangerous; Saddam lived for revenge, and that his biological weapons, in particular, were a great danger. He thought those biological weapons were meant for Americans, that they would be part of Saddam's revenge. He told me *Saddam is a destroyer.*

PBS: And what did he mean by that?

MYLROIE: I assume that he meant that Saddam, in some way, lives for destruction. I didn't ask him to explain any further. He said, "*Saddam is a destroyer.*" It's open to whatever interpretation people would put on it by destruction.[7]

There can be little doubt, regardless of what prophetic attachment one may or may not wish to associate with it, the name Saddam means "the Destroyer." And Revelation's fifth trumpet clearly defines the person or entity that brings about the devastation outlined in this prophecy as the Destroyer . . . Apollyon . . . Abaddon.

However, now we must answer the question of whether Saddam Hussein was really such a literal destroyer as the one foreshadowed in the fifth trumpet vision. If he were such a man, along with the undeniable evidence of the meaning of his name, it would seem we have a viable candidate for the fulfillment of the ominous fifth trumpet prophecy.

24

A MEDIEVAL BLOODBATH (TRUMPET 5)

Silence in the face of evil is itself evil: God will not hold us guiltless. Not to speak is to speak. Not to act is to act.

—DIETRICH BONHOEFFER

So, was Saddam Hussein merely *called* the destroyer—or was he *actually* a destroyer in practice? There certainly is no lack of material reporting Saddam's egregious violations of human rights. He became infamous for the chemical warfare used against his own people, as well as his highly publicized "rape and torture rooms."

According to the journalist Dexter Filkins, "[Saddam] murdered as many as a million of his people, many with poison gas. He tortured, maimed and imprisoned countless more. His unprovoked invasion of Iran is estimated to have left another million people dead. His seizure of Kuwait threw the Middle East into crisis. More insidious, arguably, was the psychological damage he inflicted on his own land. Hussein created a nation of informants—friends on friends, circles within circles—making an entire population complicit in his rule."[1]

Consider also this heart-wrenching report from a November 2002 *FrontPage Magazine* article:

> Once prisoners are incarcerated for disloyalty to the regime, their suffering is so great it can scarcely be described. Many are placed in solitary confinement on starvation diets. Confessions are forced from them by the most gruesome methods imaginable: They are struck with brass knuckles and wooden bludgeons; they receive electric shocks to their genitalia; scorching metal rods are forced into their body orifices; their toes are crushed and their toenails pulled out; they have their limbs literally burned off; they are slowly lowered into large vats of acid until they confess or die. Many are poisoned with thallium, which causes its victims enormous agony before they die. When these prisons periodically get overcrowded, they are "cleaned out" by means of summary executions.
>
> Frequently, confessions are extracted by torturing not only the prisoner, but his family members as well. His wife and daughters are raped, and sometimes beheaded, as he watches. His children or grandchildren – in many cases mere toddlers – are burned with cigarette butts; their eyes are gouged out; all the bones in their feet are crushed; their ears and limbs are amputated, one at a time. If no confession is forthcoming, the youngsters are slaughtered. Moreover, some of these prisons actually house the children of suspected dissidents – children younger than twelve who are packed into cells and left to rot amid pools of their own excrement, blood, and tears.[2]

Observe this statement made in 2003 by the *New York Times*, concerning the evil that Saddam Hussein leveled upon the world. Surprisingly, the left-leaning newspaper appears to have come quite close to vindicating President George W. Bush's invasion of Iraq upon the ouster of Saddam Hussein alone:

In the end, if an American-led invasion ousts Mr. Hussein, and especially if an attack is launched without convincing proof that Iraq is still harboring forbidden arms, history may judge that the stronger case was the one that needed no inspectors to confirm: that Saddam Hussein, in his 23 years in power, plunged this country into *a bloodbath of medieval proportions,* and exported some of that terror to his neighbors.[3]

The following narrative, from an article titled "The Top 5 Crimes of Saddam Hussein," paints a further detailed portrait of the murderous, maniacal *destroyer* the world knew as the president of Iraq:

As early as April 1987, the Iraqis used chemical weapons to remove Kurds from their villages in northern Iraq during the Anfal campaign. It is estimated that chemical weapons were used on approximately 40 Kurdish villages, with the largest of these attacks occurring on March 16, 1988 against the Kurdish town of Halabja.

Beginning in the morning on March 16, 1988 and continuing all night, the Iraqis rained down volley after volley of bombs filled with a deadly mixture of mustard gas and nerve agents on Halabja. Immediate effects of the chemicals included blindness, vomiting, blisters, convulsions, and asphyxiation. Approximately 5,000 women, men, and children died within days of the attacks. Long-term effects included permanent blindness, cancer, and birth defects. An estimated 10,000 lived, but live daily with the disfigurement and sicknesses from the chemical weapons.

Saddam Hussein's cousin, Ali Hassan al-Majid was directly in charge of the chemical attacks against the Kurds, earning him the epithet, "Chemical Ali." . . .

On August 2, 1990, Iraqi troops invaded the country of Kuwait . . . As the Iraqi troops retreated, they were ordered to light oil wells on fire. Over 700 oil wells were lit, burning over one billion barrels of oil and releasing dangerous pollutants into the air. Oil pipelines were also opened, releasing 10 million barrels of oil into the Gulf and tainting many water sources. The fires and the oil spill created a huge environmental disaster.[4]

There can be no doubt that Saddam Hussein was an *Abaddon/ Apollyon*. His name, Saddam, remember, is the ancient Persian word for *the Destroyer*. His mother gave him the name, his enemies gave him the name, historians gave him the name, researchers gave him the name, politicians gave him the name, his victims lived the fury of his name, and history plainly crowns him with the name—and not just the name . . . but also the *deeds* the notorious name implies. How could this striking biblical reference, and this name identification, simply be a mere coincidence of history? Many prophecy watchers believe it plainly cannot be simple chance. Numerous Bible students are convinced *Saddam* "the Destroyer" Hussein was the Abaddon/Apollyon of Revelation 9.

In verse 4 of the prophecy, the antagonists were told not to harm the grass of the earth or any plant or tree, but only those people who did not have the seal of God on their foreheads. The "seal of God" on certain people's "foreheads" would seem to be a spiritual protection of the mind and soul for believers in Christ living in that prophetic theater, in other words, those who are "sealed for the day of redemption" (Eph. 4:30). There appears to be a promise that the military encroachment leveled upon these people would not utterly decimate the area—even though that was the ultimate goal of The Destroyer. Not only that, but there seems to be a promise to the Christians, living through this taste of hell, that no spiritual harm would come to them.

Few commentators agree specifically on the meaning of this verse so, as a matter of integrity, I will not stretch definitions to attempt to *fit* words and descriptions found in the prophecy to my view. I am merely offering a plausible interpretation in light of everything else we know about the prophecy and the word meanings found herein.

It appears Saddam Hussein is a viable candidate for the "king" who caused unprecedented destruction, gloom, suffering, and terror in this vision. He brought his demonic brand of terror up from the depths of the earth—along with fire, smoke, and deep darkness. His hate-created darkness covered the land for ten months. The sun and moon refused to shine, even in the middle of the day. The demonically spiritual nature of what Saddam wrought upon the globe during those months was a topic of discussion in coffee shops and church Bible studies the world over. And do not forget, the entire affair started with a *five-month* invasion of a tiny, oil-rich nation. That is where it began—but the effects of that initial invasion continue to reverberate throughout the world, in unprecedented fashion—even at the writing of this book. And that is not all.

As reported in the chapter titled "Unprecedented," the *New York Times* claims the subsequent Iraq war of 2003 (initiated by Saddam's Gulf War of 1991) was actually the true beginning of the infamous Arab Spring (March 2011) uprisings all over the Middle East. Many prophecy watchers believe the final results of the Arab Spring may lead to the fulfillment of trumpet number six—a huge, multinational war centered in the Middle East—some call it World War III. If this is true, the connected chain reaction originally initiated by the Gulf War and Saddam Hussein, followed by the events of 9/11 and beyond, can clearly be seen—certainly qualifying this as a possible *trumpet event* of prophecy.

In another striking correlation, some have pointed out that the particular reference from Revelation that identifies the name of the king as the "Destroyer" just happens to be chapter 9, verse 11 . . . think 9/11. Admittedly, chapters and verses were not included in the original text of the Bible when it was first penned; however, this certainly is a notable and eerily surprising association, especially in light of the fact that, not long after 9/11 occurred, none other than Saddam *the Destroyer* was targeted for attack by the Coalition forces.

AND OUT OF THE SMOKE—LOCUSTS CAME DOWN . . .

Bible readers and expositors note the unmistakable imagery of trumpet five's *locusts* filling the skies and covering the earth. They, seemingly, come out of the fire and out of the smoke itself. Perhaps coming over the horizon, the indescribable objects looked as if they had literally appeared out of the ground, or had crawled out of the Abyss itself. It appears John was, again, attempting to describe something he could not imagine. Perhaps he saw a massive invasion of tanks and various other war machines crawling and roaring across the smoke-filled desert floor. Maybe he was also describing modern attack-helicopters filling the blackened, acrid sky. How utterly dreadful these iron-plated locusts, swarming upon the earth and eerily punctuating the sky, must have appeared to John!

How else might John have described a fleet of helicopters (widely used in the Gulf War), with men's faces peering through the windshields? To an ancient man thrust thousands of years into the future, the whirring chopper blades could certainly have appeared as "the hair of women" on top of these locust-things, and the armament and heavy equipment adorning these unthinkable machines of war may easily have looked like "crowns" and "the teeth of lions" (vv. 7, 8). Was there any way a first-century man could describe the tails (guns and cannon turrets) that sting and torment men, other than saying they were "like unto scorpions"? (v. 10). What words would *you* have used, what imagery would you have employed, had you been in John's place?

The death, the agony, the hellishness, the devastating military technology before John's eyes—all may very well have been the same that our own generation saw in late 1990 and early 1991 in the Middle East—most of us never dreaming that we might have been witnessing an event of biblically prophetic proportions.

25

MEN WILL LONG TO DIE (TRUMPET 5)

All day and night you would hear terrible screams, and some were from children.

—ABID HUSSAN, *former prisoner of Saddam Hussein*[1]

erhaps now we can better understand the particular words in verse 6 of the trumpet five prophecy: "During those days men will seek death, but will not find it; they will long to die, but death will elude them" (Rev. 9:6 NIV).

These words have perplexed Bible scholars for almost two thousand years. Several fanciful interpretations have been brought forth, even those suggesting some kind of yet-unknown technology that artificially sustains life, even in an unwilling subject. But in light of our understanding of Saddam the Destroyer, could it not simply mean exactly what it says? Might it be a hint of the hideous torture that Saddam inflicted upon his own people, for decades? Could it be that these words allude to the indescribable chambers of horror fiendishly operated by Saddam and his regime—purposely keeping victims alive for years simply to inflict more and more levels of suffering upon them?

Can you not imagine the many thousands of people, including children and entire families, barely existing under this horror, who longed to die—yet were not allowed to do so? Many now believe this interpretation to be an incredibly good possibility. This particular explanation certainly lines up with the facts of the matter, which continue to pour in—even many years after Saddam's own death:

> BAGHDAD—Pictures of dead Iraqis, with their necks slashed, their eyes gouged out and their genitals blackened, fill a bookshelf. Jail cells, with dried blood on the floor and rusted shackles bolted to the walls, line the corridors. And the screams of what could be imprisoned men in an underground detention center echo through airshafts and sewer pipes.
>
> "This is the place where Saddam made people disappear," said an Iraqi soldier named Iyad Hussein, 37, describing Iraq's Military Intelligence Directorate in the northwestern suburb of Kadimiya. "It is a chamber of death." . . .
>
> . . . "I was beaten, refrigerated naked and put underground for one year because I was a Shiite and Saddam is a Sunni," said Ali Kaddam Kardom, 37. He said he was arrested in the central city of Karbala on March 10, 2000. He returned to the facility in Baghdad this weekend, [April 13, 2003] he said, to help rescue any Iraqis who still might be imprisoned there. . . .
>
> An Iraqi soldier, who according to the facility's records witnessed the beatings, said interrogators regularly used pliers to remove men's teeth, electric prods to shock men's genitals and drills to cut holes in their ankles. . . .
>
> "I have seen interrogators break the heads of men with baseball bats, pour salt into wounds and rape wives in front of their husbands," said former Iraqi soldier Ali Iyad Kareen.[2]

These many years later, the innumerable stories of Saddam's holocaust of terror inflicted upon his own people are still told. Perhaps none are more heart wrenching than the tales of the screams and cries of mere children suffering at the hands of Saddam's sadistic henchmen. Here is one macabre account:

> ABID HUSSAN took one step inside the foul-smelling prison cell and began to shake. Beads of sweat ran down his forehead and behind his gold-rimmed spectacles. The 45-year-old shopkeeper pointed to the electric cables hanging from the ceiling where President Saddam Hussein's security police would torture him three times a day. . . .
> . . . "They held me in this stinking hole for ten months," he said.
> He lifted his shirt to show the scars and weals on his painfully thin legs where he had been whipped with electric cable. "All day and night you would hear terrible screams, and some were from children."[3]

Following is an excerpt from an article titled "Prisons for Children Discovered in Baghdad":

> On April 8, the French news service AFP reported that U.S. marines had liberated a children's prison in Northeast Baghdad. The report said that 100 to 150 children poured out of the unlocked prison gates and swarmed around their marine liberators. A marine officer told an AFP embedded reporter that the children looked undernourished and were wearing threadbare clothing.
> Ironically, these children may have been the lucky ones. Over the past decade, international organizations like Human Rights Watch, have repeatedly reported on the imprisonment, torture, and execution of children by the Saddam Hussein regime. Children have been among the nearly 300,000 persons who have "disappeared" in Iraq since the later 1970s. Children have been routinely and repeatedly arrested to force their parents to confess to crimes against the regime.
> For example, a March Boston Globe story detailed the interrogation of a former Iraqi secret police thug who had specialized in

torture. The thug admitted torturing children as young as five or six to "get their mothers talking." He claimed that Iraqi torturers never killed the children, just "beat them with steel cables."[4]

Can you not imagine that most of these children, after some time, longed for the sweet release of death? We cannot begin to fathom the agony of the parents of these little ones, unable to rescue their children from the hands of this sociopath madman—perhaps wishing, and even praying, for the mercy of death for their own children. This horror is too unimaginable for most of us to even consider. Yet, there were thousands who had to *live* it, under the regime of "the Destroyer."

In June 2002, a BBC correspondent had this to say regarding the torture of children in Iraq under the Destroyer's reign of abject terror: "In northern Iraq—the only part of the country where people can speak freely—we met six other witnesses who had direct experience of child torture, including another of Saddam's enforcers—now in a Kurdish prison—who told us that an interrogator could do anything: 'We could make a kebab out of the child if we wanted to.' And then he chuckled."[5]

It is not surprising to discover that an ever-increasing number of prophecy students are interpreting this previously difficult verse (Rev. 9:6) as the desperate desire of the people of Iraq and Kuwait to escape—even by death—the excruciating and horror-filled times in which they lived under the madman Saddam Hussein. They suffered greatly, beyond adequate description, during his reign of wretched medieval terror. Might not at least a few of them have begged for death?

The long-awaited execution of Saddam Hussein took place on Saturday, December 30, 2006. Saddam the Destroyer was sentenced to die by hanging after being found guilty by the Iraqi Special Tribunal of *crimes against humanity*. In the end, Saddam's trial and ultimate execution were infinitely more merciful than the brutal punishment he inflicted upon the people of his own country.

COINCIDENCE, OR PRECISE PROPHECY?

Consider again the prophecy of the fourth trumpet. That vision predicted the world would grow measurably dimmer in the last days – an unprecedented one-third event. Could it be that the Bible was speaking of the scientifically calculable dimming that would occur in our current time, a fact that has been reported around the world for decades?

And is it a coincidence that trumpet five predicts that a people would be tormented, for a specific period, by a Destroyer who would unleash fire and locusts from the "Abyss"—and that the Kuwaitis suffered for *precisely* that period under Saddam *the Destroyer* and his war machines?

But that is not the end. Now it is time for *trumpet six.*

26

RELEASE THE FOUR ANGELS!
(TRUMPET 6)

The number of the mounted troops was two hundred million. I heard their number.

—JOHN THE REVELATOR[1]

O f those who believe we are now living in the trumpet days of Revelation, I am unaware of any, as of this writing, who seriously believe that trumpet number six has already been fulfilled, though many suppose we may be right on the verge of its fulfillment.

Trumpet six apparently speaks of a great multinational war that will take place in the region through which the Euphrates River traverses. Of course, this location is squarely in the heart of the Middle East.

The Euphrates is the longest river in the Middle and Near East region. It is also one of the most historically significant. Along with the Tigris, it is one of two rivers that define the region many scholars refer to as "the cradle of civilization." The Euphrates originates in northeast Turkey. The mighty river then flows down through Syria and Iraq. There it joins the Tigris, eventually emptying into the Persian Gulf.

Obviously, this is a biblically significant area and appears to be the central *region* or *theater* for the ominous sixth trumpet fulfillment. Regardless of one's specific eschatology or hypothesized timing of the rapture, prophecy students have long recognized this particular trumpet revelation as a potential World War III scenario to be played out in the very last days. This theater is the area where many believe humankind's days upon the earth began. Apparently, according to this prophecy, the humanistic and satanic philosophy of *last-days* rule will culminate in this area as well.

In the case of trumpet six, we can only speculate on the meanings and possible fulfillments—even though there certainly are some detailed clues and key words in this prophecy as well. The problem, though, is that this prophecy has not yet occurred. It is much more difficult, therefore, to make an unequivocal assertion. However, let us observe the words of the prophecy and then attempt to give credible meaning to some of the clues:

[13] The sixth angel sounded his trumpet, and I heard a voice coming from the horns of the golden altar that is before God.

[14] It said to the sixth angel who had the trumpet, "Release the four angels who are bound at the great river Euphrates."

[15] And the four angels who had been kept ready for this very hour and day and month and year were released to kill a third of mankind.

[16] The number of the mounted troops was two hundred million. I heard their number.

[17] The horses and riders I saw in my vision looked like this: Their breastplates were fiery red, dark blue, and yellow as sulfur. The heads of the horses resembled the heads of lions, and out of their mouths came fire, smoke and sulfur.

[18] A third of mankind was killed by the three plagues of fire, smoke and sulfur that came out of their mouths.

[19] The power of the horses was in their mouths and in their tails; for their tails were like snakes, having heads with which they inflict injury.

[20] The rest of mankind that were not killed by these plagues still did not repent of the work of their hands; they did not stop worshiping demons, and idols of gold, silver, bronze, stone and wood—idols that cannot see or hear or walk.

[21] Nor did they repent of their murders, their magic arts, their sexual immorality or their thefts.

—REV. 9:13–21 NIV

Since I am not willing to be dogmatic in insisting that what we have covered thus far, from trumpets one through five, is an absolute fulfillment of prophecy in our own historical lifetime, I am certainly not going to insist upon a rigorous interpretation of this sixth trumpet prophecy—which unarguably has not yet occurred. However, I will put forth some food for thought concerning at least a few of the elements of the prophecy.

At the very least, we can say the sixth trumpet prophecy declares that there are mighty and spiritual powers at work in this region of the world—particularly in the last days. Of course, we know the Islamic world currently has its seat of dominance in this theater of world events. This area is also the seat of Islamic terrorism, which continues to spread throughout the world. Additionally, it would appear that the binding of these forces is the work of God's power alone. These evil forces would be allowed to wreak their havoc only in the last days and only when the Lord decrees it, on a specific day and at a specific hour.

It is also worthy to note that the Bible plainly declares that this region, where the Euphrates River has its beginnings (Turkey), is the very place of Satan's earthly throne!

To the church in Pergamum . . . I know thy works, and where thou dwellest, even where Satan's seat is: and thou holdest fast my name, and hast not denied my faith, even in those days wherein Antipas was my faithful martyr, who was slain among you, where Satan dwelleth.

—REV. 2:13

Undoubtedly, the theater of trumpet six is indeed a demonically spiritual place. It certainly appears to be a place where angels would be released, ready to kill.

Perhaps the most striking key word here involves the number of the troops. John said, "I heard the number of them." He gave us the number 200 million. This is a staggering, unprecedented number of troops in a single theater. Even World War II did not have this many troops, although, as referenced earlier, reliable sources estimated that some 200 million troops *and* civilians, in total, were involved in that war.

Remember, also, the death toll for World War II is often estimated at 60 million or more. Again, 60 million is approaching about *one-third* of 200 million. Undoubtedly, we see shades of another great World War in trumpet six. Except this time, this final war of the ages will be tremendously more devastating than even World War II.

The Greek words John used here are significant. He was literally saying, "Their number was *two myriads of myriads*" (*Strong's Greek* #1417: *duo* and #3461: *muriadoon* [singular]). A *muriadoon* is ten thousand. So the number that John saw was *two* ten thousands times *one* ten thousand. This number is interpreted in most English translations as 200 million. The Greek word *muriadoon* is derived from the Greek root *murias* or *myrias*, the word from which we derive our English word *myriad*, an uncountable multitude.

There has been much speculation as to how 200 million troops could be staged upon a battlefield by any one standing army of today's world. Of course, this particular number, if meant to be a literal count, could refer to the combined multinational forces amassed in the region for this war of wars. However, we are only speculating at this point since the prophecy has not yet occurred.

Numerous teachings on this particular trumpet vision mention modern China's potential to produce a 200 million–man army. Many of these treatises cite a supposed statement by chairman Mao Tse-tung, sometime in the 1960s, claiming to be able to field a 200 million–man army. Therefore, a number of prophecy watchers see China as having a definitive role in fulfilling this prophecy in the last days.

While I have yet to find an exact quote from Mao Tse-tung making such a claim, I have found authoritative resources that would lend a degree of credibility to the claim. It is a documented fact that China's military force, the People's Liberation Army (PLA), is the world's largest military force, with the strength of approximately 2,250,000 personnel (about 0.18 percent of the country's population).[2] Though this is a staggering number of *ready-to-go* troops, it is still only about 10 percent of the total number of troops referenced in this prophecy.

However, observe these comments from the 1960s, reportedly made by Mao Tse-tung, which were then explained by some of his staunch supporters. The following is from the English-translated *Peking Review*:

> The People's Liberation Army should be a great school. In this great school, our armymen should learn politics, military affairs and culture. After the socialist education movement is over, they can always find mass work to do, so that *the army will forever be at one with the masses.* They should also participate in the struggles of the Cultural Revolution to criticize the bourgeoisie whenever they occur. In this way, *the army* can concurrently study, engage in agriculture, run factories and do mass work . . .While the main activity of the workers is in industry, they should *at the same time also study military affairs,* politics and culture. . . . While the main activity of the peasants in the communes is in agriculture . . . , they, too, should at the same time *study military affairs.* . . . This holds good for students too. While their main task is to study, they should . . . learn other things, that is . . . *military affairs.*
> —MAO-TSE-TUNG[3]

The obvious goal of the Chinese government and military is to make every able-bodied citizen a viable member of its army . . . ready to *go to arms* when called upon. This fact is borne out in the same *Peking Review* article by the commentator who expanded on Mao's above statement: "By acting in accordance with what Comrade Mao Tse-Tung has said, it will be possible to *turn all the people into soldiers* and greatly strengthen our combat preparedness. Should imperialism dare to invade us, it will be drowned in the great ocean of people's war."[4]

If China were to turn *all the people into soldiers* today, what kind of army, albeit low-tech, could it field? Today, China's population hovers at around 1.35 billion people. Two hundred million able bodied soldiers, out of a total citizenry of well over a billion people (imported to a field of operation in the Middle East) is not a far stretch of the imagination.

THE 200 MILLION-MAN ARMY OF THE MIDDLE EAST

There are those, however, who point out that it is not necessary for China to be involved in any way whatsoever for the fulfillment of trumpet six to take place. It appears the Middle East alone is quite capable of fielding such an immense "army" in the event of a geo-political calamity of biblical proportions in that area of the world.

It is a statistical fact that close to 400 million people live in the Middle East today.[5] Of those 400 million, almost 320 million are Muslim.[6] Islam is the dominant religion in all of the Middle Eastern states except Israel and the Palestinian areas.

Given the undeniable fact that the sixth trumpet prophecy opens up within the heart of the Middle East and more than likely has something to do with a war centered around the restored nation of Israel, it is not hard to imagine that a 200 million–person fighting force could quickly arise in this region of the world. Considering that Islamic forces do not hesitate to use women and children in combat roles, the scenario is even likelier. This prophetic development is made even more conceivable with the probability that the

United States and various European nations would be involved in a war of this magnitude and importance. When one adds in the possibility of China and/or Russia being implicated in this war—200 million combatants is a highly plausible and easily attainable number.

There is no small number of fanciful interpretations from various prophecy commentators as to what the colors (red, yellow, blue) mean and what the images of the beasts are, upon which the riders are mounted. We cannot know these meanings with certainty because they have not yet happened. Remember: if trumpet number three truly was the Chernobyl nuclear disaster of 1986, it still would have been impossible for anyone to know the exact meaning of that prophecy until it had actually occurred.

However, here is what we *can* know about the trumpet six prophecy: a war such as the world has never seen is soon to come to the Middle East. It will have cataclysmic, worldwide effects because it is a *one-third* event. There will be a massive toll of human life. The specific theater of the battle will be at the Euphrates River and will perhaps involve, in particular, the nations through which the river traverses. It appears we can call this *the coming World War III.* Given today's demographics of the region, we can make a fair guess that the war will be Islamic driven and will focus on the destruction of Israel. This Great War will be extremely spiritual in nature and origin.

It is not hard to imagine that the world has been building to just such an Islamic World War III event for quite some time now. Let us take a moment and trace back through some of the more obvious connections.

The Treaty of Versailles, which ended World War I, was developed and proffered by Britain, France, and the United States. The blame for the entirety of the war was laid at the feet of Germany. The treaty declared that Germany was not allowed to have a standing army. Germany also had to forfeit some of its territory, and they were forced to pay for all of the war debts. Much of this debt payment came upon the backs of the overtaxed German citizens. Germany grew angry and seethed in the desire for revenge.

Adolf Hitler became chancellor of Germany in January 1933. Almost immediately he began secretly building up Germany's army and weapons. In 1934 he increased the size of the army, began building warships, and created a German air force. Compulsory military service was also introduced. Although Britain and France were aware of Hitler's actions, they were also concerned about the rise of Communism and believed that a stronger Germany might help prevent the spread of Communism to the West. When Hitler finally invaded Poland in 1939, World War II was under way. Because of this particular chain of events, many have been led to describe World War II as merely the continuation, or the extension, of World War I.

As noted earlier, World War II not only was an unprecedented war, and remains so until this day, but it brought about several unique and notable consequences. Out of World War II came the return of Israel to the world scene. This fact has fueled massive unrest in the Middle East ever since. Out of World War II arose the technology that would produce the nuclear reactor necessary for the third trumpet prophecy to be fulfilled. Of course, the Chernobyl disaster further punctuated the world's desire for energy resources that were both clean and nonlethal.

As of this writing, there have been thirty-three serious accidents at nuclear power stations since the first recorded incident in 1952 at Chalk River in Ontario, Canada. The explosions and nuclear fuel rods melting at Japan's Fukushima nuclear power plant, following the Sendai earthquake and tsunami in March 2011, have caused fears of what might happen next. On March 14, 2011, Japan's nuclear safety agency raised the nuclear alert level for Japan from four to five—still making it two levels lower than the Chernobyl disaster in 1986.[7]

And, of course, we have already examined the possible fulfillment of trumpet four in the undeniable *global dimming* phenomenon judged by most experts to have been brought on, in part at least, by increased worldwide usage of petroleum-based products.

The powerful wheels of worldwide energy-associated politics continued to grind away. Deadly oil wars threatened and loomed in the future. The totalities, and the intricacies, of the political wrangling of multinational energy negotiations are extremely complex, but they are real nonetheless. Suffice it to say that while nuclear power was once tagged as the energy hope and primary resource of the future—the unparalleled Chernobyl nuclear disaster, and its resulting and continual horrors, hampered public opinion of such a happy, nuclear-powered-life scenario. The game of jockeying for oil production supremacy among the major oil players around the world has only heightened. This indubitable and documented dynamic was a large part of Saddam's invasion of Kuwait in August 1990.[8]

Oil supremacy, according to many experts, was also the predominant factor behind the almost immediate involvement of the United States of America, and the unprecedented multinational coalition it formed. The principal effort was to halt Iraq's seizure of the precious oil supply held by tiny Kuwait.

Iraq's invasion of Kuwait appears to have started the chain reaction of events that would roll on into trumpet six and, perhaps, lead straight into the eventual days of the Antichrist and the rapture of the church, thus setting the world up for the pouring out of the final bowls of God's wrath.

A mere decade behind Desert Storm came the horrendous events of September 11, 2001. In reaction to that potentially biblical portent came Operation Iraqi Freedom and the invasion of Afghanistan. Following those events came the election of Barack Hussein Obama as president of the United States. Under Obama's watch and administration Arab Spring followed—resulting in a complex instability of the Middle East, increasing and deadly threats to Israel, elevated terrorism aimed at United States interests (at home and abroad), and a realignment of power among Arab and oil-rich Islamic nations.

In the midst of it all, Iran, Russia, and China continue to loom and jockey for world dominance and possession of oil supplies, as well as nuclear technology. Many students of biblical prophecy see these conjoined events as a recipe for disaster—a recipe for a potential and soon-coming blast from trumpet six.

27

THE ABOMINATION
(TRUMPET 7)

Forces from him will arise, desecrate the sanctuary fortress, and do away with the regular sacrifice. And they will set up the abomination of desolation.

—DANIEL 11:31 NASB

A s we move into an exploration of the seventh trumpet, found in Revelation 11, it is important to give consideration to the two verses preceding the mention of God's *two witnesses* of the last days. The verses in question draw attention to the measuring of the temple of God. Specific instructions are given regarding this measurement, and a precise associated time frame is noted. Observe these verses:

Then there was given me a measuring rod like a staff; and someone said, "Get up and measure the temple of God, and the altar, and those who worship in it." Leave out the court which is outside the temple, and do not measure it, for it has been given to the nations; and they will tread under foot the holy city for forty-two months.

—REV. 11:1–2 NASB

If John wrote the book of Revelation in the AD 90s, then the Romans had already destroyed the temple in Jerusalem when John saw the vision. The temple was leveled by Rome in AD 70. Some see this fact as a definitive indication that a new and third temple *must* be rebuilt in Jerusalem in the last days in order to complete end-time prophecy—since John specifically mentioned the temple's existence.

Others see John's vision as a spiritual *traveling back in time* to the era when the temple was still standing—for the purpose of measuring it and declaring that it (or the area of it) would be trampled upon, in some significant way, by the Gentiles in the very last days. Still others believe this passage is proof that John wrote the book before the temple was destroyed in AD 70. I am not dogmatic about any of these interpretations—however, there *is* a connection that does interest me.

Numerous students of end-time prophecy believe this passage in chapter 11 is a direct reference to something the prophet Daniel and the Lord Jesus Himself said about the temple area in the last days. Both spoke of an *abomination that causes desolation:*

And he said, "Go your way, Daniel, for these words are concealed and sealed up until the end time. Many will be purged, purified and refined; but the wicked will act wickedly, and none of the wicked will understand, but those who have insight will understand. And from the time that the regular sacrifice is abolished, and the abomination that causes desolation is set up, there will be 1,290 days.

How blessed is he who keeps waiting and attains to the 1,335 days!

—DAN. 12:9–12 NASB

Jesus actually referenced Daniel's prophecy concerning the matter of the abomination of desolation:

"This gospel of the kingdom will be preached in the whole world as a testimony to all nations, and then the end will come. "So when you see standing in the holy place 'the abomination that causes desolation,' spoken of through the prophet Daniel -- let the reader understand."

—MATT. 24:14-15 NIV

AMAZING DATE CORRELATIONS

Daniel appears to be giving God's people a formula of some sort. The formula involves specific numbers: 1,290 *days* and 1,335 *days*. It is important to note that the designation *day* in the original Greek (*hemera*, *Strong's* #2250) does allow for the symbolic interpretation of the word as *year*. Some have observed the distinct possibility, used in the context of this passage, that the term *day* is meant to be interpreted in that manner here.[1] This likelihood will be dramatically demonstrated in a moment. The numbers and clues also seem to be associated with Jerusalem and the Temple Mount. These locales would certainly qualify for the definition of the clue labeled *the holy place* (v. 15).[1]

King Nebuchadnezzar, of the Babylonian Empire, destroyed the Temple in 586 BC. The *regular sacrifice* of Daniel's day ended. If you move forward 1,290 years, starting at 586 BC, you arrive at the year AD 704–705. I hyphenate this date because I am speaking in terms of our solar calendar. The ancient Hebrews used a lunar/solar system of date reckoning.

What is significant about this time period? It just so happens that the Islamic Dome of the Rock was constructed between the years 688 and 691. The companion mosque right next to the Dome of the Rock, the Al-Aqsa Mosque, was finally completed in AD 705. This would be the exact year of Daniel's prophecy—1,290! Numerous Bible explorers have seen the precise fulfillment of the *abomination that causes desolation* in this set of date connections. It is a fact that, to both the Christian and the Jew, Islam is an abomination in several important ways. In addition, the erection of Islam's third holiest site in the world on the spot where the Temple of God used to stand surely is deemed by many to be a desecration of the ancient and original Jewish site.

Furthermore, few in today's world would argue that some of the most recent *desolations* have occurred at the hands of Islam (9/11, Arab Spring, Islamic terrorism, attacks on Israel, threats to annihilate Israel, the slaughter and devastation of Muslim-on-Muslim wars, attacks on Christians in Egypt and throughout the Middle East, and so forth).

To many Bible prophecy students, the world is now actually *experiencing* the prophecies of Daniel and Jesus. Every time there is a camera shot or video sweep of Old Jerusalem on the evening news, what is front and center in the scenery? It is the Islamic Dome of the Rock, and standing next to it . . . the Al-Aqsa Mosque. The two, many would claim, make up at least a part of the prophecy of the *abomination that causes desolation standing in the holy place.*

What is even more amazing is the fact that, at the time of Daniel's and Jesus' prophecies, Islam had not yet been founded. That would not occur until, according to the traditional Islamic view, AD 610, when Muhammad began receiving his "revelations" at the age of forty.

What about Daniel's clue of the 1,335 *days* (or years)? Numerous Bible experts have made this amazing observation: Jerusalem was recaptured and reclaimed for Israel in the year 1967. Certainly Jerusalem is the holiest city on the planet for the Jew and the Christian—and the year 1967 would be considered a *happy* or *blessed* year. Counting back 1,335 years from 1967, one arrives at the date of AD 632. That just happens to be the year of Muhammad's death (June 8, 632). Once again, Daniel's mysterious number could be seen to be directly associated with Israel, the Temple Mount, Jerusalem, Islam, and the abomination that causes desolation.

To continue the mystery further, consider this: Israel was restored in 1948, thus fulfilling a twenty-five-hundred-year-old end-time prophecy. This, obviously, is the most significant event and date in modern Israel's history. Certainly the year 1948 would be considered a year of *blessing*. Counting back 1,335 years from 1948, one arrives at the year 613. This is the exact year Muhammad began preaching his newly invented Islamic faith.[2] In other words, it would be the date of the birth of Islam. Again, we see a connection to Islam (the abomination) with Israel, Jerusalem, and everything holy to the Jew and Christian. Are these date correlations mere coincidences? Or could they be clues of precise prophecy being fulfilled as geopolitical history marches forward?

There are several other amazing numerical constructs using the mathematical keys found in the book of Daniel. Classical commentators as well as modern-day Bible experts and prophecy students have expounded these scenarios. Each has his favorite configuration for arriving at an interpretation. Some find dates corresponding to Antiochus Epiphanes of the Seleucid dynasty and his desecration outrages against the partially rebuilt temple and sacrificial system of that day. Others find dates directly associated with the coming of Jesus Christ and, particularly, His sacrifice on the cross. I am not declaring one to be more accurate than the other.

THE BOTTOM LINE

Regardless of the correlations and the varying interpretation scenarios we have just observed, the point for our study henceforth is to note the potentially prophetic message that Revelation 11:2 proclaims: "Leave out the court which is outside the temple and do not measure it, for it has been given to the nations; and they will tread under foot the holy city for forty-two months" (NASB).

The word *nation* is from the Greek word *ethnos*. This particular word means those who are not Jews, or in other words—Gentiles. Forty-two months is a period of three and one-half years—or as Daniel would have said it, "time, times, and half a time" (Dan. 7:25, 12:7 NASB). Again, there are varying interpretations of this passage, but the verse would appear, at least, to be declaring that in the very last days, even with a restored Israel in the land, Gentiles (Muslims?) would control the Temple Mount. This apparently, according to the prophecy, would remain the case until the blowing of the seventh trumpet of Revelation.

As of the writing of this book, the Dome of the Rock and the Al-Aqsa Mosque still stand upon the Temple Mount, which remains under Islamic domination. Additionally, there are continual rumblings of the potential rebuilding of a third temple on the controversial Temple Mount. Furthermore, because the abominable Islamic "witness" still stands as the foremost skyline feature of modern Jerusalem, many still see it as a harbinger of cataclysmic biblical happenings soon to come. It certainly is an abomination representing much desolation that has been caused in its name. And it is standing in an undeniably holy place.[3]

Nonetheless, at the same time, also standing as God's undeniable witnesses to the world of end-time declarations and the truthfulness of God's Word, are the revived nation of Israel and the blood-bought church of the redeemed—*the olive tree and the lampstand.*

28

WOE, WOE, WOE!
(TRUMPET 7)

"O, woe is me, to have seen what I have seen, see what I see!"
—WILLIAM SHAKESPEARE, *Hamlet*

Before we delve into trumpet seven, let me first draw your attention to an important biblical fact concerning the trumpet visions. There is a series of three "woes" that is announced in the midst of the seven trumpet announcements.

The word *woe* means "deep distress, calamity, or misery." A biblical *woe* attached to end-time prophecy would have to denote a time of unparalleled strife and confusion. Since these woes of Revelation are so specifically set apart and nestled within the trumpet visions, I believe it is important that we examine them.

Bible prophecy experts proffer various interpretations of these three woes. It appears, at the very least, they are time markers of particular importance. They seem to be signifying those events in history that would bring specific and far-reaching calamity upon the world. We first hear of the three woes announcement in chapter 8, just after the fourth trumpet has sounded: "And I looked, and I heard an eagle flying in midheaven, saying with a loud voice, 'Woe, woe, woe, to those who dwell on the earth, because of the remaining blasts of the trumpet of the three angels who are about to sound!'" (Rev. 8:13 NASB).

This passage plainly tells us the final three trumpets are, in fact, the three woes of which it speaks. Then we are told that after the fifth trumpet vision is completed, the first woe has passed—meaning the fifth trumpet was the first woe: "They have as king over them, the angel of the abyss; his name in Hebrew is Abaddon, and in the Greek he has the name Apollyon. The first woe is past; behold, two woes are still coming after these things" (Rev. 9:11–12 NASB).

The second woe announcement is connected with the "rapture" of the two witnesses, symbolically identified in Scripture as the *lampstand* and the *olive tree*. After the witnesses are lifted up into the clouds, all manner of calamity strikes in the theater of the Middle East, and perhaps Jerusalem itself.

> And they heard a loud voice from heaven saying to them, "Come up here." And they went up into heaven in the cloud, and their enemies beheld them. And in that hour there was a great earthquake, and a tenth of the city fell; and seven thousand people were killed in the earthquake, and the rest were terrified and gave glory to the God of heaven. The second woe is past; behold, the third woe is coming quickly.
>
> —REV. 11:12–14 NASB

There is no specific announcement of the arrival (or passing) of the third woe as there was with the first two woes. However, the next *woe* of which we read is not seen until chapter 12: "For this reason, rejoice, O heavens and you who dwell in them. Woe to the earth and the sea, because the devil has come down to you, having great wrath, knowing that he has only a short time. And when the dragon saw that he was thrown down to the earth, he persecuted the woman who gave birth to the male child" (Rev. 12:12–13 NASB).

Numerous students of Revelation prophecy believe the entirety of Revelation 12 to be a panoramic vignette of the revelation history of the gospel, beginning with the birth of the Christ (out of Israel—*the woman*) and continuing with His ascension into heaven and Satan's attack upon Israel and the church (there are those two witnesses again!) until the very last days of the reign of the Antichrist.

Now that we understand, from a previous chapter, that prophecy interpretation often involves a definitive ebb and flow (recapitulation) to the unfolding story—many have seen here the implication that the third woe is none other than the days of the rage of the Antichrist (Satan, who was thrown down to earth and now embodied in a man). His rage will be especially prevalent in the days following the rapture. Can you not imagine the hellish turmoil in the world in those times? The Antichrist will look foolish, and he will know that he is on his way to losing. He will be enraged beyond measure, knowing that his time is short—and that his days are numbered. The wrath of God is about to be poured out upon the earth and upon those who have been left behind. Certainly, those days will be a time of *woe*.

Examining the woes in this manner leads to several possible deductions regarding their significance and placement within the Revelation end-time prophecies. Could it be the first woe is so closely connected with trumpet five because it is with the blowing of that specific trumpet that the unprecedented downward spiral of cataclysmic events involving the Middle East began? Many see it that way. After all, if trumpet five commenced with the Gulf War and then was followed by (with definitive connections) 9/11, the Iraq and Afghanistan wars, increased Islamic terrorism, Arab Spring, and the alignment of biblical nations opposing the existence of Israel— certainly the days of trumpet five would constitute a declaration of *woe* upon the earth.

The second woe would thus be connected to the rapture of the saints in the last days. With that cataclysmic event will certainly come all manner of distress upon the earth, such as the world has never before witnessed.

The third woe I have already examined. It appears to be the final, agonizing, intolerable days of the Antichrist's rule and the pouring out of God's unmitigated wrath—the seven bowls (or vials) of wrath.

The placement of these three woes, as corresponding with the last three trumpets and beyond, is to declare the relative rapidity with which these trumpets will occur.

This is not to say the first four trumpets are not cataclysmic events. After all, if these four represent World War I, World War II, the Chernobyl nuclear disaster, and worldwide global dimming—it is difficult to dismiss these as merely minor events.

However, World War I began in 1917. World War II began in 1939. Chernobyl occurred in 1986. The Gulf War commenced in 1991. There is a time span of seventy-four years between the events of the possible first trumpet and the beginning of the possible fifth trumpet. On the other hand, the Gulf War also *ended* in 1991. Arab Spring commenced in 2011. The difference between these two events, and every cataclysmic thing that came between them (9/11, the Iraq and Afghanistan wars, increased Islamic terror, antagonistic alignment of nations against Israel, etc.), is a period of only twenty years. One can clearly observe the apparent *speeding up* of prospective end-time events as potentially represented between trumpets five and six alone. This truth brings to mind the words of the prophet Daniel in his vision of the very last days: "And its end will come with a flood; even to the end there will be war; desolations are determined" (Dan. 9:26 NASB).

Also consider the mournful and ominous words of the prophet Zephaniah as he was given a glimpse, a vision, of the end-time events of Revelation and the last days:

¹⁴ Near is the great day of the LORD, near and *coming very quickly*; listen, the day of the LORD! In it the warrior cries out bitterly.

¹⁵ A day of wrath is that day, a day of trouble and distress, a day of destruction and desolation, a day of darkness and gloom, a day of clouds and thick darkness,

¹⁶ *A day of trumpet and battle cry*, against the fortified cities and the high corner towers.

¹⁷ And I will bring distress on men, so that they will walk like the blind, because they have sinned against the LORD; and their blood will be poured out like dust, and their flesh like dung.

¹⁸ Neither their silver nor their gold will be able to deliver them On the day of the LORD's wrath; and all the earth will be devoured in the fire of His jealousy, for He will make a complete end, indeed a terrifying one, of all the inhabitants of the earth.

—ZEPH. 1:14–18 NASB; *emphasis added*

Certainly, one can see the significance of the biblical placement of these specific three woes within the Revelation trumpets. If the understanding we are examining in this book is anywhere near the correct interpretation of the Revelation trumpets, then we are currently living in the days of the first woe. Judging by existing world affairs, numerous students of the Word of God would consider that a fair assessment.

29

COME UP HERE!
(TRUMPET 7)

And they heard a loud voice from heaven saying to them, "Come up here." Then they went up into heaven in the cloud, and their enemies watched them.

—JOHN THE REVELATOR[1]

n the interpretation scenario we are examining in this book, it would be predominantly understood that the seventh trumpet represents the rapture of the church. There are several important reasons for this analysis. Since I have already developed the major elements necessary to arrive at this particular interpretation, I will only briefly review them here while, at the same time, expanding upon elements not yet explored. Let us begin by examining the seventh trumpet as it is presented in Revelation 11:

¹¹ But after the three and a half days the breath of life from God came into them, [the two witnesses] and they stood on their feet; and great fear fell upon those who were watching them.

¹² And they heard a loud voice from heaven saying to them, "Come up here." And they went up into heaven in the cloud, and their enemies watched them.

¹³ And in that hour there was a great earthquake, and a tenth of the city fell; seven thousand people were killed in the earthquake, and the rest were terrified and gave glory to the God of heaven.

¹⁴ The second woe is past; behold, the third woe is coming quickly.

¹⁵ And the seventh angel sounded; and there arose loud voices in heaven, saying, "The kingdom of the world has become the kingdom of our Lord, and of His Christ; and He will reign forever and ever."

—REV. 11:11–15 NASB

It appears that concurrent with the seventh trumpet of Revelation there is a rapture event of some sort. The rapture language of this text cannot be denied. There is the mentioning of a voice calling from heaven: "Come up here." Next, there is the description of the *witnesses* going up into the clouds while the enemies of God's people are left behind, watching in horror. And of all things, this entire event is accompanied by the seventh and *last trumpet* blast from heaven. Then we hear more voices in heaven declaring that Jesus' triumphant reign is soon to occur. The only other scriptures in the entire Bible that use this specific language and imagery are those passages directly linked to the rapture of the church. Observe this scriptural truth from the mouth of Jesus: "And then the sign of the Son of Man will appear in the sky, and then all the tribes of the earth will mourn, and they will see the Son of Man coming on the clouds of the sky with power and great glory. And He will send forth His angels with a great trumpet and they will gather together His elect from the four winds, from one end of the sky to the other" (Matt. 24:30–31 NASB).

Now, observe the apostle Paul's description of the rapture. We will hear from him in two different places within the Scriptures:

> For this we say to you by the word of the Lord, that we who are alive, and remain until the coming of the Lord, shall not precede those who have fallen asleep. For the Lord Himself will descend from heaven with a shout, with the voice of the archangel, and with the trumpet of God, and the dead in Christ will rise first. Then we who are alive and remain will be caught up together with them in the clouds to meet the Lord in the air, and so we shall always be with the Lord.
>
> —1 THESS. 4:15–17 NASB

> Behold, I tell you a mystery; we will not all sleep, but we will all be changed, in a moment, in the twinkling of an eye, at the last trumpet; for the trumpet will sound, and the dead will be raised imperishable, and we will be changed.
>
> —1 COR. 15:51–52 NASB

In these three passages, which are traditionally interpreted to be declarations of rapture truth, we find mention of the rapture being accompanied by a trumpet blast (specifically, the last trumpet), a voice from heaven, being called up and caught up, a gathering in the clouds, and the promise that we shall forever be with the Lord. These are the identical elements found associated with the seventh, and last, trumpet of Revelation.

When one further considers the fact that the two witnesses being "raptured," after seemingly much persecution in the last days, are identified clearly as the olive tree and the lampstand in Revelation 11, you can probably understand how numerous prophecy students envision a clear presentation of the rapture of the church in this last trumpet blast.

Those opposed to this particular interpretation often hold to the view that the two witnesses are literal men. Some scenarios even name the men as Moses and Elijah. Others name Enoch and Elijah.

This would seem contextually unlikely. The scripture itself does not directly identify the witnesses as literal men, nor does it name any particular men as the witnesses.

The closest this passage comes to implying that the two witnesses might be human beings is the description in verse 8 of the dead *bodies* of the witnesses. Of course, with all the obvious symbolism already being used in this portion of Revelation, it would not be unreasonable to suggest that the bodies to which this passage refers are a symbolic representation of the entity represented by the olive trees and lampstands. Before we proceed further, let us observe the actual words of the passage:

> ³ "And I will grant authority to my two witnesses, and they will prophesy for twelve hundred and sixty days, clothed in sackcloth."
> ⁴ These are the two olive trees and the two lampstands that stand before the Lord of the earth.
> ⁵ And if anyone wants to harm them, fire flows out of their mouth and devours their enemies; so if anyone wants to harm them, he must be killed in this way.
> ⁶ These have the power to shut up the sky, so that rain may not fall during the days of their prophesying; and they have power over the waters to turn them into blood, and to smite the earth with every plague, as often as they desire.
> ⁷ When they have finished their testimony, the beast that comes up out of the abyss will make war with them, and overcome them and kill them.
> ⁸ And their dead bodies will lie in the street of the great city which mystically is called Sodom and Egypt, where also their Lord was crucified.
> ⁹ Those from the peoples and tribes and tongues and nations will look at their dead bodies for three and a half days, and will not permit their dead bodies to be laid in a tomb.
> ¹⁰ And those who dwell on the earth will rejoice over them and celebrate; and they will send gifts to one another, because these two prophets tormented those who dwell on the earth.

[11] But after the three and a half days the breath of life from God came into them, and they stood on their feet; and great fear fell upon those who were watching them.

[12] And they heard a loud voice from heaven saying to them, "Come up here." Then they went up into heaven in the cloud, and their enemies watched them.

—REV. 11:3–12 NASB

Now let us examine the major elements of this highly cryptic portion of Revelation prophecy:

In verse 3, we are told the witnesses will prophesy for 1,260 days. This is a period of three and a half years by Jewish reckoning (360 days in a year). Another way of stating this time period is "forty-two months" (11:2 NASB). Of course, three and a half years is the midpoint of a seven-year period. Thus, many see this scene as falling in the midpoint of the time of Great Tribulation, which is commonly interpreted to be a seven-year period. The symbolism of the sackcloth is important. It is the clothing of mourning and grief. The representation here is that during this particular time of their witnessing, there will be great calamities upon the earth, and the witnesses will fall under intense persecution. If the witness is the redeemed church, as we explored earlier, then one can see how some biblical scholars draw from this particular passage a mid-tribulation rapture of the church.

Verse 4 identifies the witnesses as the olive tree and the lampstand. We have already done a lengthy study of these words and their biblical definitions. This is the only specific identification we are given of the two witnesses. They are not called *men*—and no names are given . . . they are simply called *olive trees* and *lampstands*.

Verses 5 and 6 appear to speak of the anointing of the Holy Spirit power the witness(es) will possess, especially in the very last days—most especially during the time of tribulation (great distress). The world will hate the witnesses all the more because of their displays of heavenly power and anointing—possessing the obvious favor of God's hand. Interestingly, it is in verse 6 that the NIV 1984 edition and the HCSB version translate the verse "These men have the power . . ." The word *men* is not in the original Greek text. However, the word *these* does appear in the masculine form, but this does not require that the word *men* be inserted. For this grammatical reason, the King James, the New American Standard, and the New King James versions do not include the word *men* in their translations. The NIV's (1984 edition) insertion of the word *men* in this verse appears, to some, to be more of a *commentary* on the verse or an *interpretive aid* than a strictly literal interpretation of the Greek text. We must also note that verse 10 includes in the description of the two witnesses the word *prophets*. Some have taken this as evidence that the witnesses are two literal men. However, it can also be construed that the use of *prophet* is merely a description of the *activity* of the witness (the redeemed church) in the last days—that of prophesying and proclaiming the soon-coming judgments of God.

Verse 7 appears to imply that when their period of heavenly appointed witnessing is over (corresponding with the three and a half years), the beast will unleash his full fury upon the witnesses. This is the first use of the word *beast* in the book of Revelation. The next use is found in chapter 13, where we come to understand that the beast is the Antichrist. Letting the Bible interpret the Bible, we learn that the beast of chapter 11 is the Antichrist, along with his political system (kingdom) of world dominance. He is also attached to a religious system, and person, of worldwide persuasion (the false prophet). Together, they are the driving forces behind an incredible persecution of God's witnesses in the last days.

Verses 7 and 8, taken together, seem to be speaking of an apparent victory over God's witnesses as the Antichrist exacts his vengeance upon them. He makes war with them. This will probably be through blasphemous utterances, anti-Christian legislation, the swaying of world influence against God's people, executions, imprisonment, the restricting of Christian liberties, etc. There are varying interpretations of the identification of the mystical city from whence come the anti-Christian decrees and persecution orders. Of course, Jesus was crucified in Jerusalem (although the authority for the crucifixion came from Rome). Accordingly, many interpret this verse to indicate the Antichrist will use Jerusalem (or Rome) as his seat of power and authority in the final days.

Verses 9 and 10 speak of a worldwide celebration of the destruction of the influence of God's witnesses in the last days. People actually exchange gifts to celebrate—perhaps, some believe, to purposely mock the Christian celebration of Christmas.

Verses 9 and 11 each include the identifier of three and a half *days*. This also has been an important point of debate and interpretive discussion. The time period appears to be linked to the amount of time that the witnesses will be put down, or killed, or silenced. However one might wish to interpret the matter, the witnesses *will* suffer for a period, and their influence will be temporarily halted. Since this passage also began, in verse 3, with a three-and-a-half year period, many see these designations as one and the same. This could be a legitimate way to interpret the matter since the designation *day* in the original Greek (*hemera, Strong's* #2250) allows for a figurative interpretation of the word as *year*.[2] If this time period is interpreted figuratively for *years*, you can see how other prophecy interpreters come up with a post-tribulation rapture from this passage. Interpreted in this light, the passage would appear to indicate the witnesses are prophesying mightily and, perhaps, even identifying and pointing out the Antichrist to the world in the last days. This prophesying would continue for the first three and half years of the seven-year Tribulation. In the middle of the seven years, the Antichrist would gain a victory over the witnesses and would effectively silence them (kill them—*figuratively?*) for the last three and half years—after which the witnesses would be raptured.

Verses 11 and 12 tell of the previously examined rapture event of God's witnesses. Just when the world thinks it has forever rid itself of the influence of the gospel of Jesus Christ, they discover the victory is not real . . . it is short-lived. Just when it appears to the world that Christianity has been finally put down (killed) by decree and persecution, there is a resurrection of sorts. A new breath of life enters into the witnesses. They are not dead! They are not defeated! Imagine the horror of the unbelieving world as they view the surreal event. At this moment, those left behind will realize they have always been wrong in their persecution of the witnesses—for these witnesses, indeed, were the true witnesses of the glory of God.

It will be at this mournful point in human history when the godless, mocking world will finally understand the truth—but it will be too late. The seventh and final trumpet warning has sounded. God's people are gone. The wrath of God is soon to follow. The Antichrist will be filled with demonic rage and a hellish fury. His party is over. His plan has been thwarted. The war of the ages is soon to begin. And Satan knows *Who* will win this war . . . and who will lose.

For it has been written.

30
IS THIS THE END?

Hooray! Hooray! The end of the world has been postponed!

—HERGÉ, *The Shooting Star*[1]

t seems we are now left with a decision. Is the information presented in this book simply a matter of one big coincidence—or are there serious questions of specific prophecy fulfillment at stake? There are sober students of the Word of God who see it both ways. While I am not willing to be dogmatic to the point of excluding fellowship with believers in Christ who happen to be of a different persuasion, I tend to believe we may be dealing with unfolding prophecy.

We must be careful not to make the mistake the Pharisees made. We would not want to have a bevy of potential biblical signs, keys, and clues right before our eyes and then summarily deny them or ignore them simply because they do not fit a preconceived understanding of prophecy interpretation.

So you see, the question at this point, given the preceding facts, is this: If the Bible really is the infallible Word of God, and if God really is *all-knowing*, and if prophecy is given to us so that we might not be left in the dark in the last days, then would this all-knowing God really allow His infallible and perfect Word to be polluted with such monumental coincidences only to confuse the saints of God in the last days? I have a hard time believing they are mere coincidences. American author Emma Bull says, "Coincidence is the word we use when we can't see the levers and pulleys." What say you?

PROPHETIC TIMES?

Regardless of your assessment of whether or not we might be living in the actual trumpet days of Revelation, it certainly appears we are living in prophetic times.

When Christians speak of the *end of time* or the *last days*, we do so because the Bible does and because we are commanded by God's Word to do so. A full 28 percent of the biblical text deals with matters of prophecy. A large portion of those prophecies speaks of the end-times and the return of the Lord.[2]

It is understandable that the unbelieving world is not comfortable with the message that the world may soon be coming to an end. However, that does not make the uncomfortable message less true. Remember, before 1948 even much of the *Christian* world could not fathom how Israel would be able to return to the land, but they *did* return. God's Word spoke it as certain and settled prophecy. The event happened, regardless of those who thought it would not. God's Word is always true. It will not return void.

When Christians speak of the soon-approaching judgment of God to the unsaved world, we should not do so with happiness, but with broken hearts and a sense of biblical urgency. We understand that a number of people will not believe. It has always been so. It was so before the Flood. It was also true before God's judgment fell upon Sodom and Gomorrah, and it was true in the days of Pharaoh during Moses' time. But believe it or not—God's Word *will* be fulfilled . . . eventually.

As believers, we take comfort and encouragement in the promise that the Lord will return—regardless of how we interpret the specific prophecies of Revelation or where we fall in our understanding of the rapture's timing. When Jesus *does* return, humankind's wicked rule will end, and Jesus' glorious reign of righteousness will begin. Let us unashamedly encourage one another and warn the world with these words of truth.

Regardless of whether Jesus' return occurs in our lifetime or not, there will be an end to this worldly life for each of us, perhaps sooner than we expect. We will all leave this world, either in the rapture of the church or in the natural process of death. We will all appear before our Creator and give account of what we did with Jesus' claim upon our lives.

In the meantime, we watch. We must be ready. We must discern the times around us. We must search the Scripture and pay close attention to world events that are unfolding before our eyes.

We must also prepare for and invest in our future, and live our day-to-day lives as though His return may be another one thousand years from now. On the other hand, we must proclaim our faith and reach out to the world with a passion as if Jesus might return at any moment.

We are not allowed to discern the exact date of His return, but we were given distinct markers and signs. We *are* to discern the *seasons*. The day of the Lord's return should not overtake His children like a thief in the night.

> [Jesus] answered and said unto them, When it is evening, ye say, it will be fair weather: for the sky is red. And in the morning, it will be foul weather to day: for the sky is red and gloomy.

O ye hypocrites, ye can discern the face of the sky; but can ye
not discern the signs of the times?

—MATT. 16:2–3

Now, brothers, about times and dates we do not need to write
to you, for you know very well that the day of the Lord will
come like a thief in the night. While people are saying, "Peace
and safety," destruction will come on them suddenly, as labor
pains on a pregnant woman, and they will not escape. But you,
brothers, are not in darkness so that this day should surprise
you like a thief.

—1 THESS. 5:1–4 NIV

We have had the Word of God in our possession for thousands
of years. We have had many opportunities to determine its accuracy
and truthfulness. Other than the prophecies of the last days, or
the *Day of the Lord,* numerous other prophecies have already been
specifically fulfilled in ages past. Documented history bears out the
veracity and fulfillment of these prophecies.

Likewise (and this is extremely important), we have dozens of
prophecies about the *first coming* of the Christ. They include specific
prophecies about His place of birth, His time of appearance, words
of His ministry, His miracles, His vicarious death, the brutal nature
of His crucifixion, and His resurrection and ascension. All of these
prophecies were fulfilled, to the letter, in the person of Jesus Christ.
In other words, we can trust the Word of God.

If we are able to trust His Word based on the prophecies that
have *already* been fulfilled, does it not make sense that we can trust
His Word concerning prophecies that are yet to be fulfilled?

Scores of prophecies exist, from Genesis to Revelation, about
the *second coming* of Jesus, the rapture of the church, God's final
outpouring of His wrath upon the world, and the coming of a new
earth and a new heaven—a re-created paradise. No logical reason
exists to assume these prophecies will not be precisely carried
out as well. We can speak with confidence about the end of time

(mankind's time of ruling) because the Word of God speaks with confidence, with clarity, and with persistence about such matters. We are to trust His Word.

It really is that simple.

31

BUT EVERY GENERATION BELIEVED IT WAS NEAR THE END!

"You frighten me, when you say there isn't time."
"I don't see why. Christians have been expecting the imminent end of the
world for millennia."
"But it keeps not ending."
"So far, so good."

—ORSON SCOTT CARD, *Ender's Shadow*[1]

Evidence suggests that almost every generation since the time of Jesus Christ has anticipated itself to be the generation of the *end*. Because of this, numerous detractors of the biblical message have attempted to prove the New Testament documents cannot be the infallible Word of God. They claim that Peter, Paul, and John, for example, seemed to think the end was coming in their lifetimes. Yet the end did not come. Those men were mistaken, the disbeliever would say. Therefore, they would add, the Bible is wrong.

In reality, however, it is a flawed argument. Not one of these previously mentioned biblical writers named a specific day or time when the end would come. When their words are examined in proper context, they were merely calling their generation to readiness. And so must all true preachers of the Word—in every generation.

The first-century preachers proclaimed the message of readiness because they did not know with any degree of certainty when the time of the end would come. The majority of the biblical signs we look for today, to predict the times in which we live, were given by the New Testament writers themselves. Evidently, if they knew the signs for which they were to look, they were looking for them to happen within their lifetimes as well. Yet, none of those particular signs materialized within their day. They were looking for them, hoping for them, even longing for them . . . and they were *ready* for them to occur. But they did not occur.

However, several monumental prophecies *have* been fulfilled in our lifetime and *only* in our lifetime of history. This is immensely important. Let us examine a few of them.

A TWENTY-FIVE-HUNDRED-YEAR-OLD PROPHECY FULFILLED

We cannot deny that the Old Testament predicted the return of a geographical and national Israel sometime after its initial punishment and subsequent scattering among the nations. Israel *was* punished; Israel *was* scattered, and they *did* disperse among the nations for more than twenty-five hundred years. Surprising to many, the scattering and eventual return of Israel were first predicted by Moses, in the book of Deuteronomy, sometime before the children of Israel set foot in the Promised Land.

> I call heaven and earth to witness against you today, that you will surely perish quickly from the land where you are going over the Jordan to possess it. You shall not live long on it, but will be utterly destroyed. The Lord will scatter you among the peoples, and you will be left few in number among the nations where the Lord drives you. . . .

> Then the LORD your God will restore you from captivity, and have compassion on you, and will gather you again from all the peoples where the LORD your God has scattered you. If your outcasts are at the ends of the earth, from there the LORD your God will gather you, and from there He will bring you back. And the LORD your God will bring you into the land which your fathers possessed, and you shall possess it; and He will prosper you and multiply you more than your fathers.
>
> —DEUT. 4:26–27; 30:3–5 NASB

As we move through the Old Testament pages, we find this recurring theme: Israel will return to the land as a geographical nation . . . in the last days.

The prophet Ezekiel received a striking vision of this event as recorded in the book of Ezekiel, chapter 37. This passage is commonly known as the vision of the Valley of the Dry Bones. The context speaks of an epic event that would occur in the end of times and would be witnessed by the entire world. The occasion was none other than the miraculous return of Israel to the land, the rebirth of a long-dead nation.

> Then he said unto me, Son of man, these bones are the whole house of Israel: behold, they say, Our bones are dried, and our hope is lost: we are cut off for our parts. Therefore prophesy and say unto them, Thus saith the Lord GOD; Behold, O my people, I will open your graves, and cause you to come up out of your graves, and bring you into the land of Israel. And ye shall know that I am the LORD, when I have opened your graves, O my people, and brought you up out of your graves, And shall put my spirit in you, and ye shall live, and I shall place you in your own land: then shall ye know that I the LORD have spoken it, and performed it, saith the LORD.
>
> —EZE. 37:11–14

Israel was literally "born in a day." Strikingly, the prophet Isaiah recorded this fact thousands of years before it happened. And it happened in *our* historical lifetime:

Who hath heard such a thing? who hath seen such things? Shall the earth be made to bring forth in one day? or shall a nation be born at once? for as soon as Zion travailed, she brought forth her children.

—ISA. 66:8

It simply cannot be denied that the Bible foretold, thousands of years in advance, that the scattered nation of Israel would return to its land in glory. The Bible makes it clear this return would be in the *last* days.

The truly incredible thing is that while God's people waited for the promised return to the land, centuries passed, and it did not happen. As mentioned in an earlier chapter, numerous biblical commentators and scholars of the Word (before 1948) surmised that this impossible prophetic event could happen only *after* the literal return of Jesus when He set up His physical rule on the earth. They rationalized: How could millions of Jews who were scattered throughout the nations return to the land and re-create the glory of former Israel? They declared it to be an impossible thing. But it *did* happen.

On May 14, 1948, Israel declared its independence. Millions upon millions of Jews from all over the world have streamed back to their homeland. They continue to return. They are now a major nation and a major Middle East superpower with which to reckon. They are the daily focus of geopolitical and world attention as well as the central player in day-to-day Middle East affairs.

In the last twenty-five hundred years of human history, we are the *only* generation to see this astounding, and seemingly impossible, prophecy fulfilled.

THE RETURN OF ISRAEL WAS ONLY THE BEGINNING

The astonishing prophecies of Ezekiel 38 and 39 must not be ignored in this study. These prophecies, written more than two and a half millennia ago, speak of shocking and never-seen-before alignments of certain nations. A large body of biblical scholars agree that these prophecies speak of the modern-day nations of Russia, Iran, Turkey, Egypt, Sudan, Syria, Saudi Arabia, and Libya, along with other specific Middle Eastern and African nations that will join together and attack a *returned* Israel in the last days.

The prophecy declares that Israel would be strong and back in the land when this attack happens. Our historical generation has experienced the return of Israel and her place of strength and prominence on the world scene. Even now, the nations are forming these alliances. Even now they are breathing out their incessant threats and amassing nuclear weapons for the stated purpose of attacking Israel. Interestingly, almost all of these nations are now Islamic or, at least, heavily influenced by Islam. The religion of Islam did not even exist when the prophecies were written.

We are the first and only generation to see these alignments beginning to take form. In the opinion of many biblical scholars, Israel's return to the land and, subsequently, specific nations forming alliances against her, is an unquestionable prophetic signpost. However, the return of Israel is not the only sign of the *end-times*.

MORE SIGNS

In Matthew 24, Jesus' disciples asked Him when the end would come and what would be the signs. Jesus then began to list the certain signs of the last days, this one among them: "And this gospel of the kingdom will be preached in the whole world as a testimony to all nations, and then the end will come (v. 14).

This is a fairly clear pronouncement of an end-time sign, would you not agree? Consider the fact that when Jesus spoke these words, the gospel had not been fully completed. Jesus had not gone to the cross; He had not risen from the grave or ascended into heaven. The Great Commission of reaching the world with the gospel had not yet been given. Humankind had not at that time even discovered the whole world. Additionally, the technology necessary to take the gospel to the whole world had not yet been invented. Nevertheless,

Jesus claimed that when you see the gospel (completed) going (with massive communication technologies) to the whole world (once it is discovered), then you will know the end is incredibly near.

We are the *only* generation in the last two thousand years to see this undeniable prophetic proclamation materialize. In fact, it is only within the last several decades that we have possessed the *world-reaching* technologies of global communication, information, and transportation necessary for this goal to be completed. But we are now there—in the midst of Jesus' *own* prophecy of the end-times!

Today, the gospel *is* going to the entire world. The book you are reading is a small part of the fulfillment of that prophecy. And, the clock continues to tick.

TECHNOLOGICAL MARVELS—SCIENCE FICTION OR PROPHECY?

Additionally, the Bible speaks of astounding technologies that, when first written, could not have been imagined. These technologies include the ability for the *whole world* to observe things together—at once, and for the whole world to hear the gospel. The technological miracles spoken of in the Bible also include the ability for the scattered Jews from all over the world to return, *en masse,* to Israel.

The prophesied biblical technologies also take into account a worldwide marking system that will be used by the Antichrist in the last days. This system will evidently be used to determine who can buy, sell, and work. All of the aforementioned technologies were nonexistent, humanly impossible, and unimagined, when the Bible first spoke of them.

We now routinely use television, radio, Internet, and satellite technologies. Credit cards, computer chips, holographic imaging, GPS tracking systems, digital video technology, instant and world-wide social networking technologies, and personal cell phones are a part of our everyday life. Watching news events unfolding live on an hour-by-hour basis are merely mundane parts of our lives. Jet airplane and high-speed interstate travel are routine. We seldom give any of these a second thought.

Numerous Bible students believe that every one of these technologies may have been alluded to in the Bible, thousands of years before they were invented. We now live in a world in which all of these technologies are being used to one extent or another. We are the *only* generation in human history to see these things happen. They were mere science fiction when they were described. Today, they are reality . . . *our* reality.

One may not be sold on the idea that the actual *trumpet days* spoken of in Revelation are occurring in our historical lifetime, but it would be practically impossible to deny the foregoing evidence of the fulfillment of end-time prophecy.

THE ONLY BOOK

Consider also that the Bible is the only source in the world to contain such strikingly accurate and undeniably fulfilled prophecies. And we are *living* most of them! No other faith system comes close to producing such prophecies. The Islamic Qur'an, the Hindu writings, the musings of Buddha, the works of Nostradamus, the astrology charts in the daily paper—nothing in all of history even approximates the wondrously fulfilled predictions that are found in the Word of God . . . the Holy Bible.

When one also considers that the Bible contains many other prophetic utterances that have come to pass down through the ages, documented in external historical records, the biblical track record becomes increasingly reliable. Furthermore, when the dozens of Old Testament prophecies of a *coming One*, containing the specificities of His life, ministry, crucifixion, and resurrection, are added into the mix . . . the Bible unquestionably stands uniquely alone in declaring, *thus saith the Lord.*

When we also take into account other potential end-time prophecy markers, occurring only in our unique historical time period, the possibilities become even more exciting. Today mainstream Christian media sources report that Muslims are having dreams and visions of Jesus as Messiah.[2]

Additionally, it is a well-known fact that Israel's most venerated rabbi, 108-year-old Yitzhak Kaduri, left a startling death note revelation in 2007 that was posted on Kaduri's website by his ministry organization. *News First Class* and *Israel Today* reported on the note and posted screen captures of Kaduri's cryptic message. The Kaduri note proclaimed the name of Messiah as Yehoshua, or Jesus. Rabbi Kaduri was not simply an obscure elderly rabbi tucked away in the bowels of Jerusalem. More than 250,000 people attended his 2006 funeral, and the president of Israel even gave the eulogy. As of late 2014 eleven of Kaduri's own rabbinical training school students were professing believers in Jesus Christ as Messiah as a result of Kaduri's teachings and revelations.[3]

In 2012 Messianic Rabbi Jonathan Cahn shocked the world with his book *The Harbinger.* Cahn draws striking parallels to certain Old Testament scriptures and key words within those scriptures, potentially pointing to God's judgment on America as expressed through the terrorism events of September 11, 2001.[4]

Regardless of where one stands on the issue of specific *trumpets-prophecy* interpretation being found within the pages of Revelation, an honest student of the Bible, and of history, cannot deny the enormous prophetic events that have only, and rather recently, occurred within our generation of history. We truly are living in biblically prophetic times—and some would say, the times of God's *final warning,* which leads me to the message of the remaining two chapters.

32

A NEW WORLD COMING

When I stand before God at the end of my life, I would hope that I would not have a single bit of talent left, and could say, "I used everything you gave me."

—ERMA BOMBECK

n 1947, in Grand Rapids, Michigan, evangelist Billy Graham conducted his very first crusade. In January 2013, he made the Gallup Poll's top ten list of Most Admired Men—for *the fifty-sixth time* since 1955—more than anyone else in history.

In October 2013, Reverend Graham conducted an exclusive interview with a popular online news service. At the time, he was in the process of preparing for what he called perhaps his "last crusade." In the interview, Dr. Graham related that America is drenched in a "sea of immorality" and suggested that the second coming of Christ was close at hand.[1] The following article, which covers that interview, shares more fascinating insight from the elderly, but still lively, Dr. Graham, whom many consider a prophet for our day and time:

> [According to Dr. Graham,] the Bible says that there "will be signs pointing toward the return of the Lord."
> "I believe all of these signs are evident today," Graham wrote, adding that "the return of Christ is near."
> "Regardless of what society says, we cannot go on much longer in the sea of immorality without judgment coming," he says.
> . . . This month, Graham is launching a video series that will be part of a national Gospel-presentation program called "My Hope America."
> Graham shared with Newsmax that "My Hope America" may be his last Gospel outreach.
> "It could perhaps be my last message," he wrote, "which is this: Christ is our hope for today and our promise for tomorrow. And it is fulfilled in the great work he did for mankind on the cross when he paid the penalty for our sin."[2]

Dr. Graham's interview revolved around the publishing of his most recent book, titled *The Reason for My Hope: Salvation.* Observe the striking words of end-time prophecy given by Dr. Graham during this interview:

> What a time to take the news of the day in one hand and the Bible in the other and watch the unfolding of the great drama of the ages come together. I would not want to live in any other time. The Bible speaks powerfully of trouble ahead with storm warnings that carry a booming jolt of truth. . . . We are at a crossroads, and there are profound moral issues at stake. It is time to return to biblical truth. The warning is clear; prepare to meet thy God—followed by the voice of the gentle Shepherd—the Lord Jesus—saying, "Come to Me all you who labor and are heavy laden, and I will give you rest" (Matthew 11:28 NKJV). A new world is coming. It is time for the people of the world to turn to God.[3]

Regardless of varying points of eschatology upon which we may or may not agree, can we not agree together, along with Dr. Graham, that the pervasive message of the book of Revelation is that, in the end, the people of God *win*? We win because Jesus wins. And because Jesus is completely victorious—there is a new world coming! Perhaps it will all begin very soon. It could be that the trumpets of final warning are now blowing. Even so, Lord Jesus, come . . . and come quickly!

Are you ready?

33

ALL RISE!

I intend to live forever. So far, so good.

—STEVEN WRIGHT, *American comedian*

f, at the end of the day, you are uncertain of where you stand with the eternal Lord of glory . . . please continue reading. This chapter is for you.

I spent a number of years in the field of law enforcement before the Lord called me into full-time gospel ministry. Consequently, I spent a good deal of time in and out of judicial chambers, states attorney offices, and courtroom proceedings. I have given sworn testimony as a law enforcement officer in numerous civil and criminal cases. I have firsthand knowledge of the power possessed by a judge. From the initial cry of the bailiff—"All rise!"—to the final gavel at the passing of a sentence . . . the authority is ominous. I have witnessed a sentence of death pronounced, and I have visited Florida's death row and spoken directly with the notorious rapist and serial killer Ted Bundy (executed on January 24, 1989).

All these memories bring to mind a biblical scene that is beyond any stretch of the imagination. It is that of the *final* judgment, where we *all* must answer, before *the Judge*—the Supreme Judge of the universe—to whom we must give an ultimate account. The fact of this judgment is an eternal one. It is an inescapable truth. Consider the following biblical declarations; these are only four of many:

> For we shall all stand before the judgment seat of Christ.
> —ROM. 14:10

> It is appointed unto men once to die, but after this the judgment.
> —HEB. 9:27

> But I say unto you, It shall be more tolerable for Tyre and Sidon at the day of judgment, than for you.
> —MATT. 11:22

> And I saw a great white throne, and him that sat on it, from whose face the earth and the heaven fled away; and there was found no place for them. And I saw the dead, small and great, stand before God; and the books were opened: and another book was opened, which is the book of life: and the dead were judged out of those things which were written in the books, according to their works. And the sea gave up the dead which were in it; and death and hell delivered up the dead which were in them: and they were judged every man according to their works. And death and hell were cast into the lake of fire. This is the second death. And whosoever was not found written in the book of life was cast into the lake of fire.
> —REV. 20:11–15

The coming judgment of God is an inevitable and divine appointment. We shall *all* pass from this life in death, and then give an account to our Creator. Therefore, the ultimate question of life is: *Where will you spend eternity?* God has several significant and eternal things to say regarding this question.

The message of God's love for you, and His plan for your life, is not complicated. God first wants you to understand that you *do* have a purpose in life. You are not merely a cosmic accident or a *souped-up gorilla*. In reality, you represent the crowning glory of all God has ever created.

God desires for your life to be lived with meaning, purpose, value, and dignity. He wants you to walk with Him in a personal way, through His Holy Spirit, so your life will be used to bring glory to Him and to reach others for His kingdom. However, the Bible is also clear that you cannot accomplish God's ultimate purpose for your life apart from His hand of grace.

The reason you cannot achieve salvation on your own is because you possess a sin nature. All of humanity is in this predicament of original sin. We are hopeless and lost; we are sinful beings. Within our core nature we have the propensity to reject the Word, the way, and the will of God as He has revealed it to us. And worse, the Bible asserts that our unredeemed sin nature will keep us forever separated from God's eternal love and presence.

For all have sinned and fallen short of the glory of God.
—ROM. 3:23

The wages of sin is [eternal] death.
—ROM. 6:23

But the message of hope, the *gospel* (or the good news) is this: God has provided for your salvation. He has taken this great and astonishing, merciful, and gracious feat upon Himself, providing a way for you to be restored to Him so your purpose in life and eternity may be accomplished. Your sin nature has been atoned for. It has been covered and forgiven. This was done through the perfect sacrifice of Jesus Christ, the Son of God. He alone is God's exclusive plan of salvation for humanity.

But you might ask: how can it be that God has taken upon Himself my salvation?

The Bible declares that the Word became flesh. God dwelt among us—as a man. We beheld our Creator . . . in the flesh. In the person of Jesus Christ, the Judge of the universe took off his robe, became as we are, and then paid the penalty we so deserve. He paid it *Himself*! Unbelievable, but true . . . that's why His offer of love is called *salvation.* And He did this unthinkable act of kindness . . . for *you.*

God has been *merciful* to you—He has withheld from you what you deserve . . . eternal death. He has been *gracious* to you. He has offered you something you do not deserve . . . eternal life through Jesus Christ.

But the offer is only given through Jesus. He was the only one willing to stand in your stead—and to pay the price for your sin at Calvary's cross. Your salvation will be provided through Jesus Christ, or not at all. It is your choice.

The gift of God is eternal life through Jesus Christ our Lord.
—ROM. 6:23b

Neither is there salvation in any other: for there is none other name under heaven given among men, whereby we must be saved.
—ACTS 4:12

Jesus saith unto him, I am the way, the truth, and the life: no man cometh unto the Father, but by me.
—JOHN 14:6

Please understand, you must respond to God's offer of salvation in a personal manner. It cannot be *conferred* upon you. Salvation cannot happen for you only because you *believe* in God. You are not saved merely because you read this chapter in this book.

You must personally call upon the name of the Lord Jesus to be saved, admitting you are a sinner and in need of salvation. You must be willing to repent of (turn from) your sin and to turn your life (and sin nature) over to the lordship of Jesus Christ.

You must then proclaim that Jesus Christ died for your sin and believe that He rose from the grave, proving He is the Lord of life and the exclusive way of salvation.

> That if thou shalt confess with thy mouth the Lord Jesus, and shalt believe in thine heart that God hath raised him from the dead, thou shalt be saved. For with the heart man believeth unto righteousness; and with the mouth confession is made unto salvation.
>
> —ROM. 10:9–10

Once you have settled this matter with God and have called upon the name of the Lord Jesus for your salvation, you can be assured of your inheritance in His kingdom, both in this world and in the life to come.

If you have not already done so, why not take this moment and pray to God for your salvation—right now? Why not call upon the name of the Lord Jesus Christ? You can settle this eternal matter in this very moment. The question of your salvation is the *ultimate* question of life.

> For whosoever shall call upon the name of the Lord shall be saved.
>
> —ROM. 10:13

After you have asked Jesus for His free and gracious gift of salvation, confess Him before the world.

> Whosoever therefore shall confess me before men, him will I confess also before my Father which is in heaven. But whosoever shall deny me before men, him will I also deny before my Father which is in heaven.
>
> —MATT. 10:32–33

Seek out a Bible-believing and Jesus-honoring church family. Then arrange to publicly declare, through believer's baptism, that you now belong to the Lord.

> And now why tarriest thou? arise, and be baptized, and wash away thy sins, calling on the name of the Lord.
>
> —ACTS 22:16

These are the biblical mandates. They are God's gifts to you—His offer of love, grace, and mercy. There is no greater joy, no grander purpose in life, than to be certain you are right with the God who created you, through a born-again relationship with Jesus Christ.

Welcome to God's eternal family!

NOTES

INTRODUCTION: STARTLING PROPHETIC QUESTIONS OF OUR TIME

1. David A. Patten, "Reverend Billy Graham Prepares 'Perhaps My Last Message,'" Newsmax, October 6, 2013, http://www.newsmax.com/Newsfront/Graham-evangelist-final-message/2013/10/05/id/529474/.

CHAPTER 1: I, JOHN, WAS IN THE SPIRIT . . .

1. The entirety of this chapter is presented as historical fiction. While certain literary liberties were employed along the way, it was my intention to present a highly accurate historical and biblical description of what may have taken place at John's trial and his subsequent Patmos vision. I heavily researched these matters before putting pen to paper. The historical facts and statements made within this narrative were gleaned from numerous and reliable sources of the study of Roman and biblical history during the time of John.

CHAPTER 2: I REMEMBER

1. The Samson Option is Israel's projected unleashing of the largest nuclear arsenal in the Middle East on its enemies in retaliation for an attack.
2. "Desert Storm," United States History website, accessed May 12, 2014, http://www.u-s-history.com/pages/h2020.html.

CHAPTER 3: COULD IT BE?

1. Franklin Graham 'Can't Help But Wonder' If End Times Are Near, September 4,2014. http://www.christianpost.com/news/franklin-graham-cant-help-but-wonder-if-end-times-are-near-125858/.
2. Paul Davies, "Yes, the universe looks like a fix. But that doesn't mean that a god fixed it," *Guardian* (UK), June 25, 2007, http://www.theguardian.com/commentisfree/2007/jun/26/spaceexploration.comment.

CHAPTER 4: TO RAPTURE OR NOT TO RAPTURE—*THAT* IS THE QUESTION

1. "After the Rapture, Who Are 'the Leftovers'? NPR Radio, August 25, 2011, http://www.npr. org/2011/08/25/139761867/after-the-rapture-who-are-the-leftovers.
2. David R. Reagan, "The Origin of the Concept of a Pre-Tribulation Rapture—from Man or the Bible?" Lamb & Lion Ministries, accessed May 12, 2014, http://lamblion.com/articles/ articles_rapture6.php.
3. Joel Richardson, "Rapture: Pre-trib, Post-trib, or Pre-Wrath?" Joel's Trumpet: The Ministry Website of Joel Richardson, November 5, 2013, http://www.joelstrumpet.com/?p=5464.
4. "Wolfgang Saxon," "Herschel H. Hobbs, 88, Southern Baptist Leader," *New York Times,* December 2, 1995, http://www.nytimes.com/1995/12/02/us/herschel-h-hobbs-88-southern-baptist-leader.html.
5. Herschel H. Hobbs, *Fundamentals of Our Faith* (Nashville: Broadman, 1960), 153–54.

CHAPTER 6: TRIBULATION OR WRATH?

1. 2 Thess. 2:5 NIV.
2. Shana Schutte, "Christian Persecution on the Rise," Focus on the Family, http://www.focusonthefamily.com/faith/articles/christian_persecution_on_the_rise.aspx; accessed October 4, 2013.
3. Aid to the Church in Need, *Religious Freedom in the World—Report 2010* (ACNI: 2010); available at http://esvc000174.wic001ss.server-shop.com/store/viewItem.shop?idProduct=73.

CHAPTER 7: UNPRECEDENTED

1. H. P. Willmott, World War I (New York: Dorling Kindersley, 2003), 307.
2. *Encyclopaedia Britannica*, s.v. "World War I," http://www.britannica.com/EBchecked/ topic/648646/World-War-I, accessed May 13, 2014.
3. "World War I Ended With the Treaty of Versailles," America's Story from America's Library, http://www.americaslibrary.gov/jb/jazz/jb_jazz_ww1_1.html; accessed May 13, 2014.
4. Donald Sommerville, The Complete Illustrated History of World War Two: An Authoritative Account of the Deadliest Conflict in Human History with Analysis of Decisive Encounters and Landmark Engagements (Leicester: Lorenz, 2008), 5.
5. Ibid
6. "Aviation During World War Two: Countries Involved in World War Two," Century of Flight website, accessed May 13, 2014, http://www.century-of-flight.net/Aviation%20history/ WW2/involved.htm.
7. "Chernobyl—25 Years After the Worst Nuclear Disaster in History," English Online, accessed May 13, 2014, http://www.english-online.at/news-articles/environment/chernobyl-25-years-after-nuclear-disaster.htm.
8. "How does Fukushima differ from Chernobyl?" BBC News Asia-Pacific, December 16, 2011, http://www.bbc.co.uk/news/world-asia-pacific-13050228.
9. Alan Greenblatt, "Twenty Years Later, First Iraq War Still Resonates," NPR, February 24, 2011, http://www.npr.org/2011/02/24/133991181/twenty-years-later-first-iraq-war-still-resonates. The article goes on to say, "Bin Laden was incensed that 'filthy, infidel crusaders,' as he called American troops, were based in his homeland of Saudi Arabia, home to Islam's two holiest sites. 'Bin Laden has repeatedly referred to the U.S. going into Saudi Arabia as a key reason for Sept. 11,' says [political scientist Steve] Yetiv, who has just published a history of U.S. policy toward Iraq." See also Mike Hanna, "The connection between Iraq and 9/11," Al Jazeera, September 7, 2011, http://www.aljazeera.com/indepth/spotlight/ the911decade/2011/09/201197155513938336.html; Scott Malesek, "Yes, the Iraq War and the 9/11 Attacks ARE Related," *Free Republic*, September 11, 2009, http://www.freerepublic. com/focus/news/2337428/posts; and Samuel A. Stanson, "What Actually Led to 9/11," *The Moderate Independent* (blog/online journal) 2, no. 8 (April 16–30, 2004), http://www.moderateindependent.com/v2i4911reality.htm. A quote from this article: "So let's sum up so far.

President Bush, Sr. told Saddam we didn't care one way or the other if he invaded Kuwait. So, Saddam did. As a result we launched a war. We used this war as a reason to put troops on Saudi soil. This turned Osama against us. And that . . . directly led to 9/11. It's all very simple and documented."

10. Kanan Makiya, "The Arab Spring Started in Iraq," New York Times Sunday Review, April 6, 2013, http://www.nytimes.com/2013/04/07/opinion/sunday/the-arab-spring-started-in-iraq.html?pagewanted=all&_r=0.

11. Youssef M. Ibrahim, "After the War: Another War Begins as Kuwaiti Oil-Well Fires Threaten Region's Ecology; Blazes Could Burn for Two Years," New York Times, March 16, 1991, http://www.nytimes.com/1991/03/16/world/after-war-another-war-begins-kuwaiti-oil-well-fires-threaten-region-s-ecology.html.

12. Ibid.

13. Brian Duffy and Peter Cary, "Gulf War: Why It Ended in 100 Hours," Orlando Sentinel, March 15, 1992, http://articles.orlandosentinel.com/1992-03-15/news/9203130459_1_saddam-hussein-persian-gulf-24th-infantry.

14. U.S. Department of State, Office of the Historian, "A Short History of the Department of State: The First Gulf War," http://history.state.gov/departmenthistory/short-history/firstgulf; accessed May 13, 2014.

15. Thomas G. Whittle, "Lives in the Balance," Freedom magazine 29, no. 1, p. 15, http://www.freedommag.org/english/vol29i1/page15a.htm; accessed May 13, 2014.

16. "Transcript: Part 2: The Gulf War" (transcript of Frontline show #1408T, aired February 4, 1997) Frontline website, http://www.pbs.org/wgbh/pages/frontline/gulf/script_b.html.

17. Michael Kelly, "The American Way of War," Atlantic, June 2002, http://www.theatlantic.com/past/docs/issues/2002/06/kelly.htm.

18. "PETER ARNETT: CNN and Live Coverage of War," on the website of Reporting America at War, http://www.pbs.org/weta/reportingamericaatwar/reporters/arnett/livecoverage.html; accessed May 13, 2014.

19. Kelly, "The American Way of War."

20. Sirisha Akshintala, "The Ten Largest Terrorist Attacks—Ever," List Dose, May 30, 2013, http://listdose.com/top-10-largest-terrorist-attacks-ever/; "September 11," http://www.state.gov/documents/organization/10288.pdf, accessed May 13, 2014.

21. "Iraqi Death Toll," Frontline, http://www.pbs.org/wgbh/pages/frontline/gulf/appendix/death.html, accessed May 13, 2014. See also Operation Iraqi Freedom and Operation Enduring Freedom Casualties, http://icasualties.org/; and "United States Military Casualties of War," http://en.wikipedia.org/wiki/United_States_military_casualties_of_war. This Wikipedia article is thoroughly referenced from 105 different credible and scholarly sources. The various tables in the article offer a quick synopsis of the massive amount of information presented.

CHAPTER 8: BIBLICAL TRUMPETS

1. Ariela Paleia, "What Is a Shofar?" About.com: Judaism, Jewish Holidays page, accessed May 13, 2014, http://judaism.about.com/od/holidays/a/whatisashofar.htm.

CHAPTER 9: THE FEASTS OF THE LORD AND THE BOOK OF REVELATION

1. "Rosh HaShanna One Day or Two?" YouTube video, 21:09, from an interview with HaRav David Bar-Hayim, posted by "Tora Nation Machon Shilo," August 27, 2013, https://www.youtube.com/watch?v=Ax9eb97DcoU; Rav Davidh Bar-Hayim, "Rosh Hashana—a holiday in transition," Ynet News, September 12, 2007, http://www.ynetnews.com/articles/0,7340,L-3448819,00.html.

2. The Mishnah is the first major written redaction of the Jewish oral traditions known as the "Oral Torah." It is also the first major work of rabbinic literature. "Commentary on Tractate Avot with an Introduction (Shemona perakim)," World Digital Library, accessed May 13, 2014, http://www.wdl.org/en/item/3964/.

3.   "The Talmud is a central text of Rabbinic Judaism. . . . The *Talmud* contains the teachings and opinions of thousands of rabbis on a variety of subjects . . . The Talmud is the basis for all codes of Jewish law and is much quoted in rabbinic literature." "What is 'Talmud'?" LifeSun, October 28, 2013, http://lifesun.info/what-is-talmud/.
4.   Paul Sumner, "He Who Is Coming: The Afikoman," Hebrew Streams, accessed May 13, 2014, http://www.hebrew-streams.org/works/judaism/afikoman.html#N5.

CHAPTER 11: PAUL'S MYSTERIOUS LAST TRUMPET
1.   International Standard Bible Encyclopedia (Grand Rapids: Eerdmans, 1979), 689.
2.   John Hagee, *Four Blood Moons: Something Is About to Change* (Brentwood, TN: Worthy, 2013), 90.

CHAPTER 12: UNDERSTANDING BIBLICAL REVELATION
1.   Robert H. Gundry, *Church and the Tribulation: A Biblical Examination of Posttribulationism* (Grand Rapids: Zondervan, 1973), 75.

CHAPTER 13: THE OLIVE TREE AND THE LAMPSTAND
1.   "Zechariah Sees a New Lampstand," from Ligonier Ministries, the teaching fellowship of R. C. Sproul. All rights reserved. Website: www.ligonier.org | Phone: 1-800-435-4343; http://www.ligonier.org/learn/devotionals/zechariah-sees-new-lampstand/, accessed October 6, 2013.
2.   Albert Barnes, *Barnes' Notes on the Old and New Testaments*, Heritage ed., 14 vols. (London: Blackie and Son, 1884; Grand Rapids: Baker, 1996), commentary on Zechariah 4; emphasis added.

CHAPTER 15: GONE ARE THE SOUNDS OF LIFE
1.   Carl Sagan, *The Demon-Haunted World: Science as a Candle in the Dark*, repr. ed. (New York: Ballantine, 1997), 26.
2.   Information for this account was gleaned from numerous sources on the Internet. However, the bulk of the information came from a riveting and brilliantly written article published in April 2006 by *National Geographic*, titled "Inside Chernobyl: The Long Shadow of Chernobyl" by Richard Stone, http://ngm.nationalgeographic.com/print/features/world/europe/ukraine/chernobyl-text.

CHAPTER 16: THE NAME OF THE STAR WAS WORMWOOD
1.   United Nations, "Current General Assembly Session Can Mark Beginning of New Era in United Nations History, President Tells Opening Meeting," press release GA/SM/1, September 16, 1997, http://www.un.org/News/Press/docs/1997/19970916.GASM1.html.
2.   *The Columbia Electronic Encyclopedia*, s.v. "Damocles," http://encyclopedia2.thefreedictionary.com/Damoclean+Sword, accessed May 14, 2014.
3.   United Nations, "Hennadiy Udovenko (Ukraine)—Elected President of the Fifty-Second Session of the General Assembly," undated news release, http://www.un.org/ga/55/president/bio52.htm.
4.   Ibid.
5.   United Nations General Assembly, Forty-fifth session, "Excerpts from the provisional verbatim record of the thirty-second meeting held at Headquarters, New York on Tuesday, 23 October 1990, at 10 a.m." (A/45/PV.32), http://chernobyl.undp.org/spanish/documentos/45pv32.htm.
6.   Ibid.

7. Ibid.
8. National Cancer Institute, "Higher cancer risk continues after Chernobyl; NIH study finds that thyroid cancer risk for those who were children and adolescents when exposed to fallout has not yet begun to decline," March 17, 2011, http://www.cancer.gov/newscenter/newsfromnci/2011/ChernobylRadiation.
9. J. J. Mangano, "A post-Chernobyl rise in thyroid cancer in Connecticut, USA.," *European Journal of Cancer Prevention* 5, no. 1 (February 1996): 75–81; available online at the website of the National Center for Biotechnology Information, http://www.ncbi.nlm.nih.gov/pubmed/8664814.
10. "Thyroid Cancer is on the Rise in the U.S.," *Daily News*, Special Advertorial, 2009, on the website of the New York Eye and Ear Infirmary, http://www.nyee.edu/pdf/highlights-2009i-dailynews.pdf, accessed September 24, 2013.
11. "Political Leaders Help Victims of Chernobyl Living in New York," at ibid; emphasis added.
12. "Radioactivity in Norway's reindeers hits high," The Local, Norway's news in English, October 6, 2014, http://www.thelocal.no/20141006/radioactive-reindeer-found-in-norway.

CHAPTER 17: A MERE GAME OF WORDS?

1. *Pontypool*, directed by Bruce McDonald (2009; Toronto(?): Maple Pictures, 2010), DVD.
2. "Did your Christian Leaders ever tell you made up stories at church in order to keep you faithful?" Yahoo Answers, accessed September 24, 2013, http://uk.answers.yahoo.com/question/index?qid=20110603201945AAEQjtX;.
3. MEBuckner, "What does Chernobyl mean?" "Straight Dope" message board, February 2, 2000, http://boards.straightdope.com/sdmb/showthread.php?t=37091.
4. Jimmy Akin, "Checking Suspicious Claims," JimmyAkin.com: The New Home of JimmyAkin.org, http://jimmyakin.com/2004/12/checking_suspic.html, accessed September 24, 2013.
5. Mary Mycio, *Wormwood Forest: A Natural History of Chernobyl* (Washington, DC: Joseph Henry, 2005), 6–7 .
6. Viktor Haynes and Marko Bojcun, *The Chernobyl Disaster* (n.p.: Hogarth, 1988), xi.
7. Ibid.
8. Serge Schmemann, "The Talk of Moscow; Chernobyl Fallout: Apocalyptic Tale and Fear," *New York Times*, July 26, 1986, http://www.nytimes.com/1986/07/26/world/the-talk-of-moscow-chernobyl-fallout-apocalyptic-tale-and-fear.html.
9. Jimmy Akin, "Checking Suspicious Claims."
10. Michael J. Christensen, *Knowing the Time, Annual Conference of the Center for Millennial Studies, Boston University, December 6–8, 1998 Conference Proceedings*: The Russian Idea of Apocalypse: Nikolai Berdyaev's Theory of Russian Cultural Apocalyptic, http://www.mille.org/publications/Confpro98/christensen.pdf, p. 4.
11. Bible Hub, s.v. "894. apsinthos," http://biblehub.com/greek/894.htm, accessed May 15, 2014.
12. *Wikipedia*, s.v. "Artemisia Vulgaris," http://en.wikipedia.org/wiki/Artemisia_vulgaris, accessed May 15, 2014.
13. *Wikipedia*, s.v. "Mugwort," http://en.wikipedia.org/wiki/Mugwort, accessed May 15, 2014.
14. *Wikipedia*, s.v. "Chernobyl," http://en.wikipedia.org/wiki/Chernobyl_%28city%29#Name_origin; accessed May 15, 2014.
15. Ukrainian New Testament: Easy-to-Read Version, Bible Gateway, http://www.biblegateway.com/passage/?search=%D0%9E%D0%B1%27%D1%8F%D0%B2%D0%BB%D0%B5%D0%BD%D0%BD%D1%8F+8&version=ERV-UK.

CHAPTER 18: CHERNOBYL: WAS IT A SIGNIFICANT *WORLD EVENT*?

1. Bryan Walsh, "The World's Most Polluted Places," *Time*, http://content.time.com/time/specials/2007/article/0,28804,1661031_1661028_1661023,00.html; emphasis added.
2. A. V. Yablokov, V. B. Nesterenko, and A. V. Nesterenko, "Atmospheric, water, and soil contamination after Chernobyl," *Annals of the New York Academy of Sciences* 1181 (November 2009): 223–36, emphasis added; available online at http://www.ncbi.nlm.nih.gov/pubmed/20002050.

3. Richard Stone, "Inside Chernobyl," *National Geographic*, October 2013, 2, http://ngm. nationalgeographic.com/2006/04/inside-chernobyl/stone-text/2.

4. Charles Q. Choi, "Nuclear Cover Up: World's Largest Movable Structure to Seal the Wrecked Chernobyl Reactor," *Scientific American*, March 17, 2011, http://www.scientificamerican. com/article.cfm?id=worlds-largest-movable-structure-seal-chernobyl-reactor.

5. Bernard L. Cohen, *The Nuclear Energy Option* (n.p.: Plenum Press, 1990), chap. 7, "The Chernobyl Accident, Can It Happen Here?" http://www.phyast.pitt.edu/~blc/book/chapter7. html; emphasis added.

6. "Chernobyl Nuclear Accident," GreenFacts, http://www.greenfacts.org/en/chernobyl/ and http://www.greenfacts.org/en/chernobyl/l-2/3-chernobyl-environment.htm#2; accessed September 26, 2013; emphasis added. The Sami people, mentioned in the quote, inhabit the Arctic area of Sápmi, which today encompasses parts of far northern Norway, Sweden, Finland, the Kola Peninsula of Russia, and the border area between south and middle Sweden and Norway.

7. John Vidal, "UN accused of ignoring 500,000 Chernobyl deaths," *Guardian* (UK), March 24, 2006, http://www.theguardian.com/environment/2006/mar/25/energy.ukraine; emphasis added.

8. Phil Reeves, "Chernobyl Leak Threatens to Poison the Ukraine's Water Supply," *Independent* (UK), April 23, 1998, http://www.independent.co.uk/news/chernobyl-leak-threatens-to-poison-ukraine-water-supply-1154021.html; emphasis added.

9. Richard Rhodes, "Arsenals of Folly," *New York Times*, November 25, 2007, http://www. nytimes.com/2007/11/25/books/chapters/1st-chapter-arsenals-of-folly.html?pagewanted=all; emphasis added.

10. Yablokov, Nesterenko, and Nesterenko, "Atmospheric, water, and soil contamination after Chernobyl," emphasis added.

11. J. T. Smith et al., "Pollution: Chernobyl's legacy in food and water," *Nature* 405, no. 141 (May 11, 2000), http://www.nature.com/nature/journal/v405/n6783/full/405141a0.html; emphasis added.

12. "Assessing the Chernobyl Consequences," International Atomic Energy Agency, http://www. iaea.org/Publications/Magazines/Bulletin/Bull383/boxp6.html; and United Nations Scientific Committee on the Effects of Atomic Radiation, Sources and Effects of Ionizing Radiation: UNSCEAR 2008 Report to the General Assembly with Scientific Annexes, vol. 2 (2011), annex D, http://www.unscear.org/docs/reports/2008/11-80076_Report_2008_Annex_D. pdf; and vol. 1 (2010), http://www.unscear.org/docs/reports/2008/09-86753_Report_2008_ GA_Report_corr2.pdf.

13. "Chernobyl Sarcophagus," Chernobyl International, http://www.chernobyl-international. com/chernobyl-sarcophagus.html; no longer accessible. The article has since been archived at http://web.archive.org/web/20101018061706/http://www.chernobyl-international.com/ chernobyl-sarcophagus.html; accessed May 15, 2014.

14. Richard Stone, "Inside Chernobyl," *National Geographic*, April 2006, p. 2, http://ngm. nationalgeographic.com/2006/04/inside-chernobyl/stone-text/2.

15. Ibid., p. 6; http://ngm.nationalgeographic.com/2006/04/inside-chernobyl/stone-text/6.

16. Choi, "Nuclear Cover Up."

17. Rhodes, "Arsenals of Folly."

18. "Nuclear Fusion In Stars: Nucleosynthesis," Enchanted Learning website, accessed May 15, 2014, http://www.enchantedlearning.com/subjects/astronomy/stars/fusion.shtml.

CHAPTER 19: WARS AND RUMORS OF WARS

1. Richard Rhodes, *The Making of the Atomic Bomb*, 25th anniv. ed. (New York: Simon & Schuster, 2012), 718.

2. Jennifer Rosenberg, "The Atomic Bombing of Hiroshima and Nagasaki," About.com, 20th Century History: Events page, accessed May 15, 2014, http://history1900s.about.com/od/ worldwarii/a/hiroshima.htm.

3. Ronald Takaki, *Hiroshima: Why America Dropped the Atomic Bomb* (n.p.: Back Bay Books, 1996), 44.

4. Ibid., 43.

5. Donald Summerville, The Complete Illustrated History of World War Two: An Authoritative Account of the Deadliest Conflict in Human History with Analysis of Decisive Encounters and Landmark Engagements (Leicester: Lorenz, 2008).
6. Robert Jay Lifton, *Death in Life: Survivors of Hiroshima* (New York: Random House, 1967), 27.

CHAPTER 20: SCORCHED EARTH

1. *Strong's (Greek Dictionary of the New Testament)*, on the Greek Dictionary (Lexicon-Concordance) web page, s.v. "G1093," http://lexiconcordance.com/greek/1093.html.
2. Paul Carell, Hitler Moves East (n.p.: Bantam, 1966).
3. "Protocol 1: Additional to the Geneva Conventions, 1977," Part IV: Civilian Populations, chap. 3, art. 54.2, http://deoxy.org/wc/wc-proto.htm; accessed October 8, 2013.
4. Treaties and States Parties to Such Treaties, "Protocol Additional to the Geneva Conventions of 12 August 1949, and relating to the Protection of Victims of International Armed Conflicts (Protocol I), 8 June 1977." ICRC (International Committee of the Red Cross), http://www.icrc.org/applic/ihl/ihl.nsf/States.xsp?xp_viewStates=XPages_NORMStatesParties&xp_treatySelected=470; accessed October 8, 2013.
5. W. Warren Wagar, *H. G. Wells: Traversing Time* (Middletown, CT: Wesleyan University Press, 2004), 147.
6. Barbara Wertheim Tuchman, *Zimmermann Telegram*, 2nd ed. (New York: Macmillan, 1966).
7. Walter Karp, *The Politics of War: The Story of Two Wars Which Altered Forever the Political Life of the American Republic (1890–1920)* (New York: Harper & Row, 1979).

CHAPTER 21: WHO TURNED OUT THE LIGHTS?

1. Kenneth Change, "Globe Grows Darker as Sunshine Diminishes 10% to 37%," *New York Times*, May 13, 2004, http://www.nytimes.com/2004/05/13/us/globe-grows-darker-as-sunshine-diminishes-10-to-37.html.
2. Ibid.
3. "Global Dimming: Horizon producer David Sington on why predictions about the Earth's climate will need to be re-examined," upd. September 2005, BBC, http://www.bbc.co.uk/sn/tvradio/programmes/horizon/dimming_prog_summary.shtml.
4. Susan K. Lewis, "Understanding Global Dimming," *NOVA*, April 18, 2006, http://www.pbs.org/wgbh/nova/earth/understanding-global-dimming.html.
5. The Met Office and Duncan Clark, "What is global dimming?" *Guardian* (UK), May 11, 2012, http://www.theguardian.com/environment/2012/may/11/global-dimming-pollution.
6. Sierra Raine, "Global Cooling Underway," American Thinker, May 7, 2014, http://www.americanthinker.com/2014/05/global_cooling_underway.html.

CHAPTER 22: OPEN THE PITS!

1. Bert Houston, "Noon Is Black as Midnight," *Dumfries and Galloway Standard and Advertiser*, March 22, 1991, http://www.angelfire.com/me/Patersonplace/page2.html.
2. David Klein, "Mechanisms of Western Domination: A Short History of Iraq and Kuwait," January 2003, http://www.csun.edu/~vcmth00m/iraqkuwait.html.
3. Joe Treen, "Fields of Fire," *People*, April 29, 1991, http://www.people.com/people/archive/article/0,,20114991,00.html.
4. Daniel Yergin, *The Quest: Energy, Security, and the Remaking of the Modern World* (New York: Penguin, 2011), http://www.e-reading.biz/bookreader.php/1010824/Yergin_-_The_Quest.html.
5. Ibid.
6. Ibid.
7. Treen, "Fields of Fire," emphasis added.
8. Houston, "Noon Is Black as Midnight."

CHAPTER 23: THE DESTROYER COMETH

1. Bert Houston, "Noon Is Black as Midnight," *Dumfries and Galloway Standard and Advertiser*, March 22, 1991, http://www.angelfire.com/me/Patersonplace/page2.html.
2. *Dictionary.com*, s.v. "Apollyon," http://dictionary.reference.com/browse/apollyon; s.v. "Abaddon," http://dictionary.reference.com/browse/Abaddon?s=t.
3. Bruce Gottlieb, "What's the Name of Saddam Hussein?" *Slate*, November 16, 1998, http://www.slate.com/articles/news_and_politics/explainer/1998/11/whats_the_name_of_saddam_hussein.html; emphasis added.
4. Peter Beaumont, "Saddam paradox divides Iraqis," *Observer*, July 3, 2004, http://www.theguardian.com/world/2004/jul/04/iraq, emphasis added.
5. Irvin Baxter Jr., "Saddam Hussein in the Bible," EndTime Ministries, November–December 2002, http://www.endtime.com/archived-magazine-articles/saddam-hussein-in-the-bible/; emphasis added.
6. "Young Shiite Firebrand Tones Down His Rhetoric," *Post and Courier*, November 10, 2003, http://news.google.com/newspapers?nid=2482&dat=20031110&id=updIAAAAIBAJ&sjid=IQoNAAAAIBAJ&pg=2519,4639672, accessed September 26, 2013, no longer accessible. See also John T. Correll, "Verbatim," *Air Force Magazine*, January 2004, http://www.airforcemag.com/MagazineArchive/Pages/2004/January%202004/0104verb.aspx.
7. Laurie Mylroie, interview by *Frontline*, PBS, October 18, 2001, http://www.pbs.org/wgbh/pages/frontline/shows/gunning/interviews/mylroie.html.

CHAPTER 24: A MEDIEVAL BLOODBATH

1. Dexter Filkins, "Regrets Only?" New York Times Magazine, October 7, 2007, http://www.nytimes.com/2007/10/07/magazine/07MAKIYA-t.html?pagewanted=2&ei=5088&en=310195565a77e9ff&ex=1349409600&partner=rssnyt&emc=rss&_r=0
2. John Perazzo, "Iraqi Horrors the 'Peace Movement' Ignores," FrontPage Magazine, November 29, 2002, http://archive.frontpagemag.com/readArticle.aspx?ARTID=20937.
3. John F. Burns, "The World; How Many People Has Hussein Killed?" *New York Times*, January 26, 2003, http://www.nytimes.com/2003/01/26/weekinreview/the-world-how-many-people-has-hussein-killed.html?pagewanted=all&src=pm; emphasis added.
4. Jennifer Rosenberg, "Top 5 Crimes of Saddam Hussein," About.com About.com, 20th Century History page, accessed May 15, 2014, http://history1900s.about.com/od/saddamhussein/a/husseincrimes.htm.

CHAPTER 25: MEN WILL LONG TO DIE

1. Daniel McGrory, "Inside The Hell of Saddam's Torture Chambers," *Times*, April 9, 2003, http://www.freerepublic.com/focus/f-news/888342/posts.
2. Jack Kelley, "Iraqis pour out tales of Saddam's torture chambers," *USA Today*, April 13, 2003, http://usatoday30.usatoday.com/news/world/iraq/2003-04-13-saddam-secrets-usat_x.htm.
3. McGrory, "Inside The Hell of Saddam's Torture Chambers."
4. Notra Trulock, "Prisons for Children Discovered in Baghdad," April 24, 2003, Accuracy in Media, http://www.aim.org/media-monitor/prisons-for-children-discovered-in-baghdad/.
5. John Sweeney, "Iraq's tortured children," BBC, June 22, 2002, http://news.bbc.co.uk/2/hi/programmes/from_our_own_correspondent/2058253.stm.

CHAPTER 26: RELEASE THE FOUR ANGELS!

1. Rev. 9:16 NIV.
2. Staff Writer, "Military Strength of China," GFP, upd. March 27, 2014, http://globalfirepower.com/country-military-strength-detail.asp?country_id=China.

3. "The Whole Country Should Become a Great School of Mao Tse-tung's Thought—In Commemoration of the 39th Anniversary of the Founding of the Chinese People's Liberation Army," *Peking Review* 9, no. 32 (August 5, 1966): 6–7, http://www.marxists.org/subject/china/peking-review/1966/PR1966-32e.htm, emphasis added.
4. Ibid., emphasis added.
5. Middle East, "Peoples," Global Perspectives website, http://www.cotf.edu/earthinfo/meast/MEpeo.html, accessed May 16, 2014. Population statistics for the figure of 400 million include the nations (and Palestinian territories) of: Egypt, Iran, Turkey, Iraq, Saudi Arabia, Yemen, Syria, United Arab Emirates, Israel, Jordan,Gaza Strip and West Bank, Lebanon, Oman, Kuwait, Qatar, Bahrain, and Cyprus.
6. Drew Desilver, "The World Muslim Population Is More Widespread Than You Think," *FACTANK* (blog), June 7, 2013, http://www.pewresearch.org/fact-tank/2013/06/07/worlds-muslim-population-more-widespread-than-you-might-think/.
7. "Nuclear power plant accidents: listed and ranked since 1952," *Datablog*, March 14, 2011, http://www.theguardian.com/news/datablog/2011/mar/14/nuclear-power-plant-accidents-list-rank.
8. F. Gregory Gause III, "The International Politics of the Gulf," in Louise Fawcett, ed., *International Relations of the Middle East* (Oxford: University Press, 2005), 263–74.

CHAPTER 27: THE ABOMINATION

1. Strong's #2250: hemera (pronounced hay-mer'-ah) feminine (with 5610 implied) of a derivative of hemai (to sit; akin to the base of 1476) meaning tame, i.e. gentle; day, i.e. (literally) the time space between dawn and dark, or the whole 24 hours (but several days were usually reckoned by the Jews as inclusive of the parts of both extremes); figuratively, a period (always defined more or less clearly by the context):--age, + alway, (mid-)day (by day, (-ly)), + for ever, judgment, (day) time, while, years. http://www.bibletools.org/index.cfm/fuseaction/Lexicon.show/ID/g2250/page/7.
2. *Encyclopedia of the Middle East*, s.v. "Muhammad," accessed May 19, 2014, http://www.mideastweb.org/Middle-East-Encyclopedia/muhammad.htm.
3. "Is Islamic Control over the Temple Mount Hampering Biblical Prophecy?" *Christian Post*, http://www.christianpost.com/news/is-islamic-control-over-the-temple-mount-hampering-biblical-prophecy-67956/.

CHAPTER 29: COME UP HERE!

1. Revelation 11:12 nasb
2. "Hemera (pronounced hay-mer'-ah) feminine (with 5610 implied) of a derivative of hemai (to sit; akin to the base of 1476) meaning tame, i.e. gentle; day, i.e. (literally) the time space between dawn and dark, or the whole 24 hours (but several days were usually reckoned by the Jews as inclusive of the parts of both extremes); figuratively, a period (always defined more or less clearly by the context):--age, + alway, (mid-)day (by day, (-ly)), + for ever, judgment, (day) time, while, years." *Strong's* #2250, Bible Tools, http://www.bibletools.org/index.cfm/fuseaction/Lexicon.show/ID/g2250/page/7.

CHAPTER 30: IS THIS THE END?

1. Hergé, *The Shooting Star* (The Adventures of Tin Tin), trans. Leslie Lonsdale-Cooper and Michael Turner (Boston: Little, Brown, 1978), 10.
2. How Much of the Bible Contains Prophecy? https://timlahaye.com/shopcontent.asp?type=FAQ.

CHAPTER 31: BUT EVERY GENERATION BELIEVED IT WAS NEAR THE END!

1. Orson Scott Card, *Ender's Shadow*, repr. ed. (New York: Tor, 2013), 58.
2. Chris Mitchell and Julie Stahl, "Dreams, Visions Moving Muslims to Christ," CBN News, February 6, 2013, http://www.cbn.com/cbnnews/insideisrael/2012/june/dreams-visions-moving-muslims-to-christ/.
3. Gallups, Carl, *The Rabbi Who Found Messiah*, (Washington: WND Books, 2014).
4. Cahn, Jonathan, *The Harbinger*, (Grand Rapids: Frontline Publishers, 2012).

CHAPTER 32: A NEW WORLD COMING

1. David A. Patten, "Reverend Billy Graham Prepares, 'Perhaps My Last Message,'" Newsmax, October 6, 2013, http://www.newsmax.com/Newsfront/Graham-evangelist-final-message/2013/10/05/id/529474/.
2. Ibid.
3. Ibid.

ABOUT THE AUTHOR

Carl Gallups is a senior pastor, best-selling author, long-time conservative talk radio host, and a much sought-after prophecy, Bible, and revival conference speaker. He is also a former decorated Florida law enforcement officer with several years experience as a deputy sheriff.

Carl has been the guest speaker in chapel services of the New Orleans Baptist Theological Seminary, The University of Mobile, and the Baptist Sunday School Board. He served as a national and international youth evangelist for over ten years with the Southern Baptist Convention Sunday School Board.

Carl has preached to thousands of people from coast to coast and internationally including Hawaii, Alaska, Canada, Israel, and Peru.

Carl is founder of the viral Internet ministry – the PPSIM-MONS News and Ministry Network. He is also the host of Freedom Friday With Carl Gallups and Ask The Preacher – both programs air over 1330 WEBY in Northwest Florida and have regional, national, and international audiences.

Carl has appeared in hundreds of radio and television markets around the nation and the world including TBN with Dwight Thompson, TBN with Pat Boone, Christ in Prophecy TV, TCT

Network, Atlanta Live, The Herman and Sharon Show, Fox News Radio with Alan Colmes, the Andrea Tantaros Show with Samantha Sorbo, The Peter Boyles Show, Janet Parshall, Coast To Coast with George Noory, Jan Markell, and many others.

The World Tribune, The Washington Times, WND.com, and other prominent publications have favorably reviewed his work. He is also a popular guest-commentator on all things biblical, prophetic, and geo-political.

Carl resides in Milton, Florida with his wife, Pam, and has been the senior pastor of Hickory Hammock Baptist Church since 1987.

CONTACT CARL GALLUPS ONLINE AT WWW.CARLGALLUPS.COM

INDEX

INDEX

C

Cahn, Jonathan (rabbi), 207
candlestick (of Revelation), 85. *See also*
    lampstand
Caron, George, 131–32
chemical weapons, 11, 158
Chalk River (Ontario, Canada), 174
Chernobyl
    meaning of the word, 91
    nuclear disaster, vii, xiv, 14, 40, 91, 95–96,
        98–101, 102, 115, 121, 128, 136, 139,
        173, 174, 175, 185
    estimated deaths 50 years after, 119
    initial number of people impacted, 117
    National Geographic report on cancer from,
        118–19
    Russian Academy of Sciences article on
        contamination after, 118
    significance of, 116–27
    as the third trumpet of Revelation, 116–27
Chernobyl Disaster, The (Haynes), 112
"Chernobyl's legacy: Health, Environmental
    and Socio-Economic Impacts," 120
children, Saddams prisons for, 164–65
China, 171–73, 175
Christ the exclusive way to salvation, xvi, 215.
    See also Jesus Christ
Christians, percentage of religious persecution
    directed at, 30
church
    God's witness to the world of Jesus Christ,
        88
    identification as the lampstand, 86
    necessary after salvation, 216
CNN, 11
Cohen, Bernard L., 119
Cohen, Shabtai, 142
coincidence, 14, 16, 115, 126, 145, 148, 159,
    166, 180, 195, 196
"Come up here" (Rev. 11), 79, 183, 187–94
confessing Christ, 216
Czechoslovakia, 119

D

Damasus I (pope), 26
Damoclean sword, comparison of "Chernobyl
    star of Wormwood" to, vii, 100, 110–11
Daniel, 70, 76, 177–80, 185
darkness. *See chap. 21* (140–45). *See also* 48,
    149, 150–51, 159–60, 186
date correlations, 178–80
David (king of Israel), 74
Davies, Paul Charles William, 16–17
Day of Atonement, 46, 51, 52

"days" (Daniel's abomination prophecy),
    177–79
death, men will seek, 147, 162–65
deaths
    50 years after Chernobyl, estimated, 119
    at the hands of Saddam Hussein, 156
    Gulf War, 13
    linked to Chernobyl, current estimate, 120
    over a five-year span from Hiroshima bomb-
        ing, 132
    resulting from World War I, 138
    resulting from World War II, 133
Destroyer, 152–60, 162, 165–66
dimming (global), xiv, 141–45, 166, 174, 188
Dome of the Rock, 178, 179, 181
dragon (as representative of Satan), 83, 184
Dubouka, Ouladzimir, 103

E

earthquake, vi, 72, 79, 174, 183, 188
Egypt, 54, 74, 179, 190, 204, 225n5
    and Moses, 34–35
Elijah (prophet), 189
Enoch (patriarch), 189
Euphrates River, 12, 167–68, 169, 173
Europe, Chernobyl accident's effects on, 119,
    120, 126

F

fake Israel, 25
false prophet, 192
feasts of the Lord, xiv, 49, 50–55
    and the book of Revelation, 50–55
    Feast of Atonement (aka Day of Atonement),
        51, 54, 55
    Feast of Firstfruits, 53
    Feast of Pentecost, 53, 88–89
    Feast of Tabernacles, 54–55
    Feast of Trumpets, 45, 49–52, 55, 67, 78
Filkins, Dexter, 156
final judgment, 211–12
Finland, 119, 120, 222n6
forty-two months (of Rev. 11), 177, 180, 191
France, 173, 174
FrontPage Magazine, 157
Fukushima, Japan, nuclear disaster, 40, 174
Fundamentals of Our Faith (Hobbs), 22

G

Gematria, 76
Gentiles as members of God's household, 87
German Tribune, 154
Germany, 133, 139, 173–74
global dimming, xiv, 141–45, 166, 174, 188

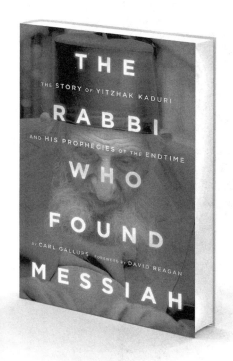
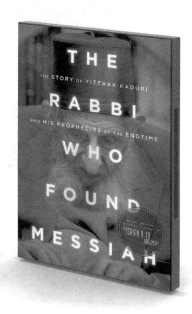

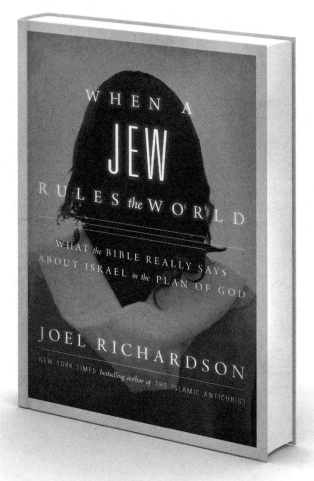

"There is a sense in the world that things are unhinged."
—JONATHAN CAHN

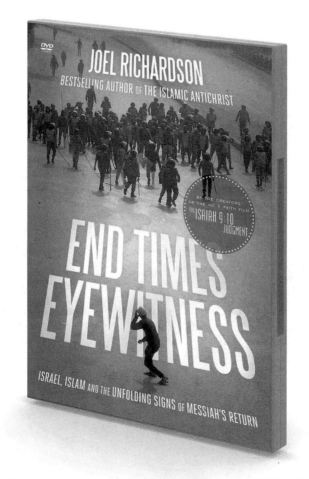

Is the return of Jesus closer than you think? What are the most powerful prophetic signs being fulfilled on the earth today? How is the new Middle East after the Arab Spring aligning with the testimony of the biblical prophets? What are the little-known prophetic signs that few are paying attention to? END TIMES EYEWITNESS takes you on a firsthand journey to the front lines of the ongoing Middle Eastern revolutions, to discover the shocking answer to all of these questions.

"*Blood Moons* is the most compelling, prophetic book of our generation."—Laurie Cardoza-Moore

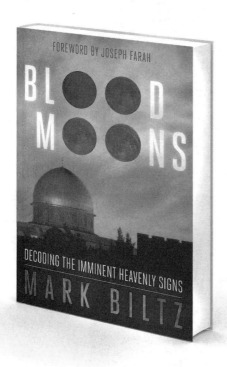
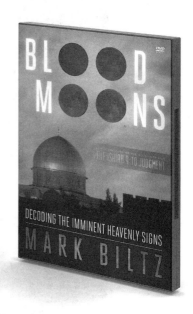

Throughout history God, the Master Timekeeper, has used the heavenly bodies to communicate to us when significant events will happen. If you want to understand the timing of the Lord, you have to understand the seasons of the Lord, the feasts of the Lord, and the calendar of the Lord. In BLOOD MOONS Pastor Biltz explains the importance of these biblical celebrations and milestones and shows how you too can be aware of the signs of things to come.